Managing People

This ⟨...⟩ exciting fourth edition of *Managing People: A Practical Guide for Front-*⟨...⟩ ⟨...⟩s addresses the growing needs of front-line managers who are not th⟨...⟩ ⟨...⟩cialists in personnel management but whose roles require them to have ⟨...⟩ ⟨...⟩ls. A growing trend over the last two decades has given these manage⟨...⟩ ⟨...⟩asing amount of responsibility of direct line management, which can be e⟨...⟩ ⟨...⟩hallenging especially if the correct training is not given.

This ⟨...⟩ ⟨...⟩ines how the different parts of managing people fit together, whilst ⟨...⟩ ⟨...⟩ng that different contexts require different approaches and recognisi⟨...⟩ ⟨...⟩g organisational, environmental and legal changes that affect the employn⟨...⟩ ⟨...⟩ework. It recognises the rapidly changing context in which modern ⟨...⟩ ⟨...⟩ managers have to operate and acknowledges the increasing expectat⟨...⟩ ⟨...⟩f good leadership as a necessity. However, the book also emphasises the nee⟨...⟩ ⟨...⟩front-line managers to understand themselves, and their own managem⟨...⟩ ⟨...⟩tyles and attitudes, together with the importance of empathy in appreciatin⟨...⟩ ⟨...⟩rspectives of the staff that work under them.

Managing ⟨...⟩ *A Practical Guide for Front-Line Managers* is designed for both new manag⟨...⟩ ⟨...⟩or NVQ/SVQ Level 4 students. It is also appropriate for the first stages ⟨...⟩ ⟨...⟩ndation Degrees and for HND courses combining academic study with ⟨...⟩ ⟨...⟩e learning.

Rosemar⟨...⟩ ⟨...⟩**son** was Senior Lecturer at The Open University Business School, U⟨...⟩ ⟨...⟩as the author of the first two editions of this book before she sadly passe⟨...⟩ ⟨...⟩n 1998. Her husband, Andrew Thomson, has worked with Eileen Arney ⟨...⟩ pr⟨...⟩ this new edition.

Eilee⟨...⟩ ⟨...⟩*y* is Lecturer in Management at The Open University, UK. Eileen has previo⟨...⟩ ⟨...⟩orked as a senior civil servant in the Home Office, including as Assistant Director of National Police Training. She has also worked in specialist HR and recruitment roles and as an executive coach.

Managing People

A practical guide for
front-line managers

Fourth Edition

**Rosemary Thomson
and Eileen Arney**

Routledge
Taylor & Francis Group

LONDON AND NEW YORK

First published 1993
Second edition 1997
Third edition 2002
By Elsevier Butterworth-Heinemann

Fourth edition 2015
by Routledge
2 Park Square, Milton Park, Abingdon, Oxon OX14 4RN

and by Routledge
711 Third Avenue, New York, NY 10017

Routledge is an imprint of the Taylor & Francis Group, an informa business

British Library Cataloguing in Publication Data
A catalogue record for this book is available from the British Library

Library of Congress Cataloging in Publication Data
Thomson, Rosemary.
  Managing people : a practical guide for front-line managers / Rosemary Thomson, Eileen Arney
  and Andrew Thomson.—Fourth edition.
    pages cm
  Includes bibliographical references and index.
  1. Personnel management.   I. Arney, Eileen.   II. Thomson, A. W. J.   III. Title.
  HF5549.T515 2015
  658.3—dc23
2014030952

ISBN: 978-0-415-71353-5 (hbk)
ISBN: 978-0-415-71354-2 (pbk)
ISBN: 978-1-315-88323-6 (ebk)

Typeset in Bembo
by RefineCatch Limited, Bungay, Suffolk

Printed by Ashford Colour Press Ltd.

Contents

7. Performance management   99

8. Managing challenging situations   117

9. The regulation of behaviour at work   135

10. Operating in a world of change   156

List of figures and tables

Figures

Tables

Acknowledgements

This fourth edition has been prepared by Eileen Arney and Andrew Thomson, husband of Rosemary. Rosie, as she was universally known, sadly died in 1998 after writing the first and second editions of this book. But the concept, the structure, the style and the spirit of the present book are still hers, and her position as lead author is still very much justified.

The authors acknowledge ideas and concepts contained in Open University Business School courses, in particular the iconic 'Effective Manager', of which Rosie was chair for several years. We would also like to acknowledge the contribution of Acas (the Advisory, Conciliation and Arbitration Service), whose common-sense and practical approach to employment matters we would hope is echoed in these pages.

1 Managing people in the twenty-first century

Introduction

Managing people is one of the most important parts of a manager's role. It can also seem the most challenging, especially for those new to line management, and of course it can also be very rewarding. People are often the most important resource in an organisation and their front-line manager can make an important difference to the way they feel about their work and the way they perform at work. In this book we will argue that it is the quality of the leadership and management provided by front-line managers which most influences the way employees feel about their organisation and their willingness to work hard to achieve its objectives – so it is a role which is critical to the organisation's success.

Providing this leadership and management is not easy. In an economic environment characterised by volatility, uncertainty, complexity and ambiguity, organisations and those who work for them must constantly find new and better ways of working to remain competitive. This means continuously learning from experience and applying that learning to changing situations. Front-line managers face this challenge themselves and also have a critical role in helping those who work for them to rise to it. The quality of their interactions with their staff makes an important contribution here and depends as much on ability to manage emotions and relationships as on more technical management skills.

By front-line managers we mean those who have taken on management responsibilities for the first time, and this book provides an introduction to current approaches to people management and the thinking behind them. However, knowing about these approaches is only the first step; the way you carry out your people responsibilities in practice is what really matters and makes the difference. For this reason we have provided throughout the text suggestions for ways of applying the ideas you have been reading about to your workplace practice.

This first chapter will give an overview of what a front-line manager needs to understand in relation to managing people in a changing environment, as well as looking at some theories about how to do this. The theme of the chapter is change and its impact on what managers do generally as well as in their role as managers of people. We will also comment on emerging research and thinking about the best ways of managing people and the importance of context. We will be looking at the following:

- what does a front-line manager do?
- changes in the external environment
- changes within organisations
- continuity
- approaches to managing people
- the importance of context
- the impact of people management practices
- skills you will need as a front-line manager
- the importance of ethics
- how to use this book.

What does a front-line manager do?

Front-line managers have a range of responsibilities, including managing budgets, work rotas, quality and operational performance (Acas 2014). However, simply listing these responsibilities does not really capture the variety and complexity of the role or the pressures it carries. Although our main focus in this book will be on people management, it is worth spending some time considering the whole span of your role and how people management fits within this. At the end of this chapter, you will be asked to undertake a diary exercise to try to capture what you actually do in your job as a manager. You will probably find that, like Sara in the case study below, you do a great deal more than might be assumed from simply looking at your formal responsibilities.

Sara works as a front-line manager in a cashier's department. She lists as her key responsibility the banking of all money received. This involves supervising administrative assistants who sort out cash, cheques and Giro pay-in slips and check these against control sheets. She is responsible for checking any discrepancies in the daily total and informing other departments when they are responsible for errors. However, the first thing she did one morning was to confirm the holiday rota with her staff; on another morning, she had to spend some time training a new recruit to the office and then attend a monthly meeting on staff appraisal; on a third morning, she had to talk to one of the clerks about persistent lateness ... and so on. None of these tasks is closely related to her key responsibility, yet they were all part of her job.

The range of work you are likely to have to deal with can include managing day-to-day relationships with your staff, dealing with attendance issues, responding to requests for flexible working and at the same time motivating your staff, managing their performance and paying attention to welfare and health and safety issues. You may sometimes have to deal with more challenging issues such as managing grievances and disciplinary matters and you will find more guidance on these in Chapter 8. You may also find that you are under pressure from more senior managers to deliver against organisational objectives. These pressures are set out in figure 1.1 below.

There have been many attempts to define what managers actually do and we will look at two very influential, but very different, approaches to this. The first, by

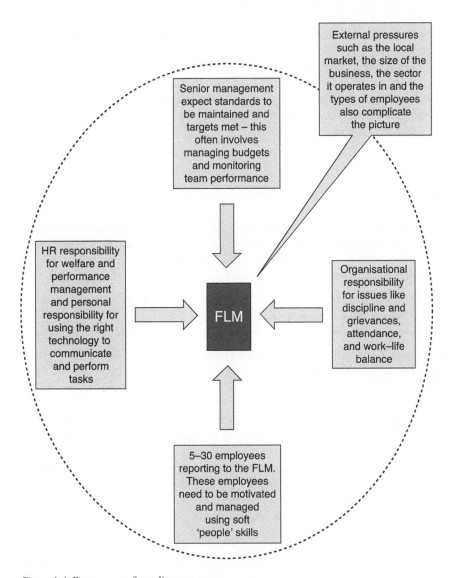

Figure 1.1 Pressures on front-line managers.

Source: Acas 2014: 2
© Acas, Euston Tower, 286 Euston Road, London NW1 3JJ

Henri Fayol, tries to explain what managers do by looking at their functions, whilst the second, by Henry Mintzberg, looks instead at the activities managers actually carry out. Whilst their accounts are very different, both can help you, in different ways, to understand the dimensions of your own role.

Henri Fayol, a mining engineer by training, spent his working life in a French mining and metallurgical combine, first as an engineer and then moving into general management, finally becoming managing director. From his prolonged observation of managers, he concluded that every managerial job contained the same five elements, although individual managers in different industries might lay more stress on some elements than on others. Writing in 1916, he identified the five elements of management as:

> *Forecasting and planning* – looking to the future; ensuring the objectives of the organisation are being met; short- and long-term forecasting; being able to adapt plans as circumstances change; attempting to predict what is going to happen.
>
> *Organising* – ensuring that the structure of the organisation allows its basic activities to be carried out; giving direction; defining responsibilities; making decisions and backing these up through an efficient system for selecting and training staff.
>
> *Commanding* – we might prefer to use the word 'leading' here since this refers to the relationship between a manager and his or her staff in relation to the task being performed including counselling, appraisal, giving feedback, allocating work and so on.
>
> *Coordinating* – ensuring that individuals, teams and departments work in harmony towards common organisational goals; keeping all activities in perspective with regard to the overall aims of the organisation.
>
> *Controlling* – ensuring that the other four elements are being carried out; operating sanctions if necessary.
>
> (Pugh and Hickson 1996)

Sara's early morning activities could readily have been classified into these elements. The holiday rota involved forecasting and planning as well as coordination; the training session required organising as did the staff appraisal system; commanding and controlling were involved in her talk with the person who was not performing adequately. However, in other important respects Fayol's account probably does not do justice to the complexity of Sara's workload or the importance for her, as for all line managers, of managing relationships in the workplace.

Mintzberg, writing in 1973, took a very different approach and used activity studies to look at what managers actually do. He found that a manager's job is characterised by a considerable fragmentation of varied and brief activities, with frequent interruptions. He found that although managers have to deal with substantial amounts of paperwork they really prefer verbal contacts, and spend a great deal of time in meetings. Pressure is created by the pace at which these activities are conducted. There is little time for reflection, and managers tend to operate to short-term rather than long-term objectives. Sara's activities seem to reflect this, given the variety of work she had to undertake in a short period of time and the ability she needed to move from one activity to another, which was quite different.

The role of managers and particularly front-line managers is a subject of considerable interest to researchers as recognition grows of the importance of their role and in particular the importance of their role in managing people. This is partly because so much people management, which was once seen as the responsibility of the personnel department, has now been devolved to line managers in general and front-line managers in particular. This means that in practice the way employees experience working for an organisation is strongly influenced by the way their line manager behaves, and since most employees are managed by front-line managers this role is pivotal. Recent research has emphasised the vital role that line managers can play when they manage relationships in the workplace in a way that engenders a good sense of morale and encourages workers to 'go the extra mile'. You will read more about what this means for the skills you will need to develop as a manager later in this chapter.

Changes in the external environment

Front-line managers' roles and the skills they need have changed in response to shifts in the external environment and this will continue to be the case as the environment continues to change. This is, arguably, happening at a faster rate than ever before in human history and some of the most important changes include the following:

- Globalisation is increasing competitive pressures from organisations throughout the world and organisations are routinely relocating all or part of their activities to facilitate access to talent, cheap labour or favourable tax regimes.
- Developments in information technology, the growing use of social media and improvements in mobile communications are changing the nature of work itself and are making it increasingly possible to work from home (or other locations remote from a central office). This in turn supports flexible working and the growth of virtual teams and work groups who may be geographically very distant from each other.
- The workforce is increasingly diverse. Demographic trends mean an older workforce in many Western countries, whilst the proportion of women in the workplace continues to rise. There is greater cultural diversity in the workforce too, partly because of migration and partly because organisations frequently span national boundaries. Many workers are only willing or able to work part time, and many will wish to be based away from the main office.
- Careers in the sense of spending most of one's working life at a single job for the same employer have, for many, been replaced by working for a number of employers, in different types of work or even being self-employed. Developing different skills requires lifelong learning and a willingness to take responsibility for continuing personal development.

- There is increasing regulation of business and working life. In Britain's case this stems largely from its membership of the European Union and much of this regulation focuses on increasing legal protection for individual rights in the workplace. At the same time trade unions, originally set up to protect workers' rights, have seen a decline in their influence in most areas of employment in the UK, with union membership in the working population falling significantly. In other words, legal protection has, in many industries, largely replaced the unions as the protector of workers' rights.

Changes within organisations

Change is a constant feature of organisational life as organisations seek to reduce costs or seek competitive advantage, and this shows no sign of abating. This means that being able to lead staff through change is a critically important skill for managers and this will be an important theme of this book.

Line managers are expected to take greater responsibility for personnel or human resource management issues while central HR units may focus only on strategic or policy-making activities. Specialist HR services such as payroll, learning and development and recruitment may be outsourced or provided by service centres shared between different units or even between organisations. This responsibility can be particularly challenging for front-line managers, who will often have no previous experience of managing people.

Many organisations have reduced the number of management layers to produce 'flatter' organisations, and this has meant an increase in the delegation of responsibility throughout the workforce, with more workers carrying out at least some managerial roles. Managers often have a wider span of control (in other words they manage more people than used to be the case) and this may include responsibility for people who are widely dispersed, supported by the use of IT.

At the same time there is extensive contracting out, with organisations retaining a smaller core of permanent workers. This means that managers may have to manage the implications for their own responsibilities of the performance of staff who do not work for them and who may not even be employed directly by the same organisation.

Within managerial roles, there is an increasing emphasis on leadership and the ability to bring out the best in staff by encouraging commitment or 'engagement'. This reflects a growing recognition, at least in organisations committed to progressive HR policies, of the importance of people as organis-ational assets and the importance of creating a sense of engagement in the workplace so staff are encouraged to make an extra effort to meet their employer's objectives. You will read more about employee engagement in Chapter 4 and leadership in Chapter 6.

Managers are expected to undertake continuous learning in the workplace as well as attending training courses and most of their learning is expected to come from the first of these. This means that they need to be able to manage their own learning and to be able to learn from experience as well as from more formal learning and development situations.

There is a strong emphasis on managing performance in the workplace and many organisations use performance management systems to integrate the various aspects of people management with the goals of the organisation. This will often include linking pay to performance.

Continuity

Having noted the prevalence of change, however, a cautionary point needs to be made. There is still a great deal of continuity; many aspects of human relations remain the same today as they have done for thousands of years since organisations became important in human evolution. What, then, remains the same? Essentially human behaviour, and it is an appreciation of what lies behind this which is at the heart of the successful management of people. Managing people is not just about making decisions and giving orders. To get the best out of them, managers need to understand and empathise with the perspectives of the people involved. Not only this, but they need to understand what lies behind these perspectives. Obviously people are different, have different values and objectives and may behave differently even in the same situation. But there are also social pressures in a group which predispose people to think and behave similarly. It is this recognition of the way individuals respond as individuals but also relate to groups and social pressures which managers need to understand. Organisations and their contexts may be changing but the essence of the relationships between people remains the same.

Applying these ideas to your own experience

How far do you see these changes in your organisation and how do they affect your practice as a manager?

Approaches to managing people

An understanding of different approaches to managing people will help you to understand your own organisation's expectations of you as a manager. You are not likely to be a specialist in personnel management, and you are not expected to be, but this section will give an overview of the way thinking about personnel management, or people management, has developed over time.

Changing approaches to managing people

The management of people in organisations began to be recognised as important in the late nineteenth century, although the emphasis was initially on employee welfare, both moral and physical, and was regarded as the responsibility of specialists known as welfare workers. By the 1920s there was a growing emphasis in the importance of efficiency in the management of work and people, and later on the development of specialist skills in people management. The Institute of Personnel Management was established in 1946 (it had previously been known as the Institute of Labour Management, which had itself replaced the Institute of Welfare Workers, founded in 1913).

In the post-war period a dominant issue in managing people in the workplace seemed to be managing tensions between unions, seen in many industries as the legitimate representatives of workers' interests, and employers and managers. The interests of workers and employers were seen as different and sometimes in conflict with each other. However, by the late 1990s, union influence in workplaces in the UK was in decline, a consequence both of the decline of manufacturing industries, which had been strongly unionised, and of a changed legislative environment, which weakened union power. In another significant change the value of the personnel profession itself had begun to be challenged and a new approach to managing people, human resource management, had started to take root.

Human resource management

You will certainly have come across the term human resource management (HRM), which is often used as an alternative to the more traditional term personnel management. This is a term which emerged into common usage in the late 1980s. Introduced in writings from the United States, it was first used to denote a strategic approach in which decisions about how to manage people were informed by and integrated with other strategic decisions about the management of the organisation. This thinking emerged from a growing realisation that in an increasingly competitive environment the motivation and commitment of the people working for the organisation would make an important difference to its performance.

There is a strong emphasis in the HRM approach on the importance of line managers in managing people and this has led to widespread devolution of people management responsibilities to them. This was in part fuelled by a growing disillusionment with the performance of personnel specialists and personnel departments in the late 1980s. However, research carried out by Purcell and others (2003) for the Chartered Institute of Personnel and Development has also shown how critical line managers' role can be in influencing the way people feel about their work and their sense of commitment to and engagement with it.

This shift in responsibility for people management has created important challenges for line managers, which will be explored throughout this book. It has also meant important changes for people management specialists. Many are now based in business units rather than in HR departments, working as business partners who provide support to line managers. Central HR departments may often be quite small, with a focus on setting policies and contributing to the development of HR strategies, while specialist HR activities are often outsourced, as noted in the previous section.

The HRM approach assumes that it is the people employed in an organisation who can give it a competitive edge and for this reason also holds that considerable attention needs to be paid to selecting and developing employees, and to organising their work in ways that increase the levels of responsibility and empowerment offered to them (Storey 2001). Underpinning the HRM approach, however, is another important and controversial assumption: that employers and those who work for them have the same interests and can be expected to support and promote the employer's interests. In this view (known as unitarism) the employee's cooperation is assumed. There is an alternative and quite widely held approach, however, which assumes that there is an inevitable conflict between the interests of employers and employees and that the latter need protection from the actions of employers, who are often motivated by profit. This is a pluralist approach, typically held by trade unions for example, who were formed originally to represent working men and women and to protect their interests in the workplace.

A classic summary of the characteristics of the human resource management approach was set out by Storey (2001):

Beliefs and assumptions

- That it is human resources which give competitive edge
- That the aim should be not mere compliance with rules, but employee commitment
- Those employees should be very carefully selected and developed

Strategic qualities

- Because of the above factors, HR decisions are of strategic importance
- Top management involvement is necessary
- HR policies should be integrated into business strategy – stemming from it and if possible contributing to it

Critical role of managers

- Because HR practice is critical to the core activities of the business, it is too important to be left to HR specialists alone
- Line managers need to be closely involved as both deliverers and drivers of the HR policies
- Much greater attention is paid to the management of managers themselves

Key levers

- Managing culture is more important than managing systems and procedures
- Integrated action on selection, communication, training, rewards, and development
- Restructuring and job design to allow devolved responsibility and empowerment

(Storey 2001)

In this book, the underlying assumptions will be that the policies and practices associated with the HRM approach as outlined above are desirable. This, as you know, strongly emphasises your role as a front-line manager of people. But it may well be that your own organisation does not subscribe to the HRM approach, or does so to only a partial extent. HRM practices may, for example, coexist with significant levels of unionisation, particularly in the public sector. Conversely, in many organisations there may be neither unionisation nor a high level of HRM practices. This is quite common in smaller organisations, particularly in private organisations in areas such as construction, retailing and the leisure industry for example. In reality a mixture of models exist. Some organisations have an HRM approach, some are unionised, some combine both these approaches and some have neither.

Guest and Conway (1999) point out that there are a large number of organisations where very little attention is given to the management of people. Although employee satisfaction is highest where HRM practices are well established, employees can be satisfied where they do not exist, as long as they have a positive experience of being managed in the workplace – for example feeling that they are fairly treated or that they can trust their managers. We do not argue that there is any one set of universal best practices. What is best for the organisation may differ for a number of reasons, not least the context in which it finds itself, and we will go on to look at the importance of context in the next section.

Applying these ideas to your own experience

Spend some time thinking about the people management practices in your own organisation. Can you identify an HRM approach or some elements of it, and/or are there trade unions represented in your workplace?

The importance of context

In this book you will find ideas and theories about how to manage people, but you will not find prescriptions about how to apply them in practice. This is because the best way of managing people depends on the context in which they are applied. Product and labour markets, the prevailing technology, the structure of the organisation, including its management hierarchy, all create some constraints on the HR policies. Small companies may have more intimate interpersonal relations than large companies, which may be a good or a bad thing. Companies which are driven by the needs of the production line require a different approach to managing people than those where the skills required are creative and individualistic. Those which are in a growth phase and where there is general optimism produce different interpersonal relations to those where there is decline, and survival and job insecurity are the order of the day. Culture matters too. Cultures differ between countries, but they can also vary considerably between organisations even in similar industries. In a large organisation you may also find that culture varies between departments, producing different values, traditions and styles of leadership. In managing people you must be sensitive to and take account of these dimensions.

This tailoring of practice to context is often referred to as a contingency-based approach. You may find, in your wider reading, that ideas and theories are sometimes presented as the only way, or the one best way, to manage people. In this book we are taking a different view and suggest that the best way of managing people depends on the context and also that there is almost always a range of choices, rather than a single solution. In other words, while context may be important, it is not a completely overriding constraint; there is always an element of choice for organisations in what they do. As you read this book we suggest that you consider critically the ideas you read about and how they can best be applied in your own organisation and role. You will find suggestions throughout the text about how you might do this.

The impact of people management practices

It is sometimes argued that there is a positive relationship between certain HR practices and organisational results, and a considerable amount of research has been carried out to establish whether this relationship really does exist and, if so, which HR practices these are. One of the best known surveys to explore this was carried out by Huselid in the United States (Huselid 1995). He analysed the impact of 13 'high-performance work practices' in areas which included performance appraisal, job design, information sharing, recruitment, training and promotion. He found that firms using these had significantly lower turnover, higher staff productivity and better financial performance in both the short and long run than firms that did not use them.

In Britain, Patterson and others (1997), in research at the Institute of Work Psychology, concluded that employee commitment and a positive psychological contract are fundamental to improving performance. Psychological contract means the unwritten understanding between employer and employee about what each owes the other, and is quite different from the written contract. Guest and Conway (2002) point out that the psychological contract depends on the sense employees have of the fairness of their employer and the trust they can place in them; they also found that an informal climate of employee involvement and consultation appears to have an important influence on performance.

These findings are now becoming cumulatively convincing in the sense that they demonstrate that people management practices do affect performance. However, there can be no complete account of what constitutes 'good' people management practice, as indicated earlier in this chapter, since the answer is likely to vary according to the context. Nor is there agreement yet between researchers even about the areas companies should pay most attention to. However, an important UK study which set out to explore the relationship between people management and performance identified a number of policies and practices which produced positive results and were linked to improved performance. These were:

*   opportunities for career advancement
*   doing a challenging job
*   having some influence on how the job is done
*   opportunities for training

- having a say in decisions that affect the job
- working in teams
- working for a firm that assists people to balance home and work
- being able to raise matters of concern
- having a boss who shows respect.

(Purcell and others 2003: 71)

The authors also pointed to the value of a clear organisational vision and values and, most importantly of all, emphasised the difference line managers made through the quality of leadership they displayed. Where this leadership was characterised by effective communication, involving staff and responding to suggestions and providing coaching and support, as well as exercising control of absence for example, performance was significantly improved (Purcell and others 2003).

Encouragingly the Workplace Employee Relations Study (WERS) does suggest that there has been a slight increase in employees expressing satisfaction (except in relation to job security) and contentment with their job between 2004 and 2011 (van Wanrooy and others 2013).

Skills you will need as a front-line manager

Many front-line managers are expected to demonstrate specialist technical skills which are specific to their profession. Nurses, police officers, teachers and scientists, for example, will have mastered high level specialist skills before taking on management roles. As managers they will need to develop a whole new range of skills, often while continuing to develop these existing specialist skills, and this can be a challenging and even daunting prospect. Traditionally, as you have seen, these management skills have include planning, organising, leading, coordinating and controlling, but as the pace of change in organisations quickens and the key role of managers in motivating staff to be fully engaged in and committed to their work is recognised, other skills have been added to this list. These include self-management and the ability to respond effectively to others. Perhaps most important of all, however, is the ability to keep learning and developing new competences and the willingness to take responsibility for doing so.

To give you a sense of the competences you may need to develop, here is a list of the typical competences which Acas suggest a front-line manager may need:

- communication skills
- people management
- team skills
- customer service skills
- problem solving
- managing risk and tolerating failure.

(Acas 2014: 15)

Your own organisation may have set out the competences it expects of its managers. These may be used for recruitment, appraisal and promotion for example. In the next chapter we will discuss ways of identifying the skills you want to develop as a manager and of managing your own learning and development.

Applying these ideas to your own experience

How well does the list of competences above correspond to those expected of managers in your own organisation?

Are there any competences you would want to add to this list?

The importance of ethics

One of the most difficult issues for managers is the extent to which ethical considerations play a part, both at an individual level and an organisational level. At the organisational level there are two conflicting perspectives. One of the main perspectives is the stakeholder approach, which argues that a range of those affected by the operations of the organisation have a legitimate interest in policies and decisions, and that account should therefore be taken of these. Those with such interests would certainly include the owners and also the employees, the customers, the suppliers, the governments under which the organisation is regulated, the communities where it operates, and increasingly the wider environment.

Very often stakeholders can exert pressure on an organisation and become a constraint on managerial choice; social legitimacy is an important concern even for very large organisations. A number of organisations have paid a heavy commercial price in recent years for behaving in ways that outrage their consumers and the wider public; one example is consumer outrage at the use by high street clothing stores of suppliers employing child labour. The solution lies in balancing the interests and priorities of shareholders and different groups of stakeholders. This is usually a pragmatic judgement, and the balance may well change over time. Financial concerns may be uppermost in organisational objectives, but they cannot be exclusive.

An alternative perspective argues that the shareholders' interests as the owners of the organisation are the only ones which should be taken into account. Moreover, the organisation will thrive or not according to whether it can please the financial markets, which essentially reflect shareholder interests. Its capacity to raise capital, to prevent itself from being taken over and to invest in the future will be dependent on whether it makes a satisfactory level of profits which can repay the shareholders' investment. If managers do not achieve these objectives they are likely to be replaced by others who conform more closely to shareholders' interests. In addition, market pressures appear to push in the same direction, so that higher efficiencies and competitive advantage are focused towards the main goal of profitability. Not to do this will result in competitive decline and ultimately collapse.

In a fast changing environment, then, how do you decide on the right course of action? In practice, few organisations have rules which dictate all courses of action; most are political entities in which decisions are significantly decentralised. In any case managers would not be managers if they did not have some discretion in decision-making over some parts of their responsibilities, one of which is likely to be in the way they manage people. This leaves managers with significant moral responsibilities. At the individual level should they follow the expectations of their employer if this means ignoring any ethical considerations? In any case it is not always clear which course of action will best meet the employer's financial or economic interests.

These are some of the perspectives that may guide behaviour:

*   acting in accordance with explicit rules
*   acting out of a sense of justice or equality
*   acting in what is perceived to be the most efficient or effective way
*   acting because of orders to follow a certain approach
*   acting because it is what others do
*   acting under pressure from interest groups
*   acting in one's personal self-interest or that of another group to which one belongs
*   acting to satisfy one's conscience
*   acting in a way which is most beneficial for most people.

All of these might be considered legitimate rationalisations for action, but none of them is likely to satisfy everyone. Most decisions must be trade-offs between different considerations and will tend to favour one set of interests rather than another. Ethical behaviour in this context is thus more a matter of having a consistent moral approach than it is making absolute distinctions between right and wrong.

Applying these ideas to your own experience

Who are the main stakeholders in your organisation (ie those affected by its operation)? Can you identify tensions between stakeholder responses to decisions you might make?

How to use this book

This book has been written to give managers the essential knowledge and understanding which will underpin their competence in managing people in practice. This involves knowledge of some of the more important research in the area and of recent developments, but it also involves recognition of what constitutes good practice in the management of people. Examples of practice, good and bad, are given throughout each chapter; most of this information is in the public domain and can be found in any newspaper or professional journal.

Each chapter consists of an introduction, setting the scene for what is to come. The main section covers research, ideas and practical examples of various topics within the subject area. It also contains a number of points where you are asked to stop reading and think about how the ideas relate to practice in your own organisation. These points are indicated by the words 'Applying these ideas to your own experience'. Where appropriate, some guidelines about relevant legal and regulatory frameworks are included.

At the end of each chapter there are some activities which you might like to try out to check your understanding of what you have read or to help you to think about how you might apply some of the ideas in your own job.

Activities

1. Over the next few days, try to keep a 'diary' of what you actually do in your job. You might find it useful to use the headings devised by Fayol for classifying the elements of management. You might need to keep a 'miscellaneous' heading for those tasks which do not immediately fall into Fayol's classification.

2. Go through the list of competences which Acas have identified that a front-line manager may need. Make a note of how competent you are in each of these areas and where necessary try to think of ways of developing or updating your competence.

References

Acas, (2014) *Front Line Managers.* Advisory booklet. London, Acas.

Guest D. and Conway N., (1999) 'Peering into the black hole: the downside of the new employment relations in the UK', *British Journal of Industrial Relations*, 37(3), 367–89.

Guest D. and Conway N., (2002) *Pressure at Work and the Psychological Contract.* London, Chartered Institute of Personnel and Development.

Huselid M., (1995) 'The impact of human resource management practices on turnover, productivity and corporate financial performance', *Academy of Management Journal*, 38(3), 635–72.

Patterson M. G., West A. W., Lawthorn R. and Nickell S., (1997) *Impact of People Management Practices on Business Performance.* London, Institute of Personnel and Development.

Pugh D.S. and Hickson D.J., (1996) *Writers on Organizations*, Penguin Business Books, Harmondsworth.

Purcell J., Kinnie N., Hutchinson S., Rayton B. and Swart J., (2003) *Understanding the People and Performance Link: Unlocking the Black Box.* London, Chartered Institute of Personnel and Development.

Storey J., (2001) 'Human resource management today: an assessment, in Storey J., (ed.) *Human Resource Management: A Critical Text*, 2nd edition. London, Thomson Learning.

van Wanrooy B., Bewley H., Bryson A., Forth J., Freeth S., Stokes L. and Wood S., (2013) *Employment Relations in the Shadow of Recession: Findings from the Workplace Employee Relations Survey.* Basingstoke, Palgrave Macmillan.

2   Managing yourself

Introduction

This book is about managing people, and in particular about how you as a front-line manager can manage those who work for you most effectively. We have already discussed in Chapter 1 how important this role is and the pressures you are likely to experience. To be effective in this role you will need to behave in ways which encourage your staff to want to work for you and for the organisation you represent. This means carrying out the many and varied people management tasks you have already read about and also behaving towards your staff in ways which leave them feeling positive about you and about the organisation, even when circumstances are difficult or when you have to challenge difficult behaviour, for example.

This means being able to manage your relationships with others, and this demands good levels of self-management and an ability to remain positive and accessible to others even when you are under pressure. Good time management will help to avoid this pressure turning into stress, and this will be easier if you can make good decisions (quickly when necessary) and manage meetings so that they make the best use of your time and others' time. Good communication skills, both in keeping those who work for you informed and listening to their views, will be an important factor in maintaining good relationships. Perhaps most importantly of all, you will need to be skilled at managing your own emotions and at reading and responding to the feelings of others. You will read more about these 'soft' skills in this chapter.

You will also read about developing your skills as a manager and particularly about continuously developing your skills through reflecting on and learning from your workplace practice and experience. You have already seen what a wide range of skills you need as a manager and it takes time and commitment to develop these so that you can carry out your people management responsibilities as professionally as your other operational commitments. You will also need a good understanding of your own strengths and weaknesses if you are to be effective in managing your personal and career development.

In this chapter we will be looking at various aspects of managing yourself, including:

- soft skills
- managing your time
- managing your workload
- managing stress
- making decisions
- managing meetings
- communicating
- active listening
- developing yourself
- managing your career
- managing your manager.

Soft skills

As a front-line manager you can make a considerable difference to the way those who work for you feel about their work, not just because of the things that you do but because of the way you do them. In the many interactions you will have with your staff every day you will have the opportunity to have a positive effect on the way they feel about their work – and about you as a manager. The same is true of your interactions with your colleagues, your manager and your customers. This is not just a question of being nice to people. Sometimes as a manager you will have to exercise control or to introduce measures which are unpopular, but even in these situations the way you manage yourself can have a significant effect on the outcomes of your behaviour. All this in turn depends on how well you are able to manage your own feelings and your relationships with others. These are often referred to as soft skills and are fundamentally important skills for any manager.

To manage your impact on others you need to understand the effect of your behaviours and even of your emotions on them and to manage your behaviours and emotional responses accordingly. It helps to be empathetic, that is to be able to understand and respond to the reactions of others and to be good at relationship building. You will have a better impact on others too if you can be a good model in the workplace of motivation and commitment. None of this is necessarily easy given the competing pressures you are likely to face in the workplace.

A leading writer in this field was Daniel Goleman, author of a bestselling and very influential text on 'emotional intelligence' (Goleman 1996). He identified four components of emotional intelligence:

- self-awareness – being aware of your own moods and your impact on others
- self-management – being able to control emotions and not be taken over by negative moods
- social awareness – using empathy to understand and respond to others' feelings
- relationship management – includes relationship building, communication skills and dealing positively with conflict.

(Adapted from Goleman 2001)

Seeking feedback in the workplace can help you to get a better sense of how well you are practising these aspects of emotional intelligence and how others experience your behaviours. You may find that you are naturally gifted with emotional intelligence (and perhaps you know this already). If you are not, being aware of the areas you need to improve is an important first step towards doing so. Coaching can be a good way to start developing strategies for improving your skills.

Managing your time

People often procrastinate because a particular piece of work is boring or unpleasant. One solution to this is to set aside one hour a day – often the first hour at work – to deal with all the jobs you would like to put off. Not only does this ensure the jobs are done but it can result in feelings of satisfaction and achievement at having completed them.

Most managers have to deal with a vast number of emails and perhaps also paperwork too. It is easy to feel overwhelmed and to let these pile up. One approach is to never open an email or pick up a piece of paper without doing something with it. You will also find it easier to keep control if you have a good filing system for those things you need to keep, whether this is online or in paper folders. The rest can be promptly deleted, shredded or otherwise discarded.

Setting priorities is an integral part of planning your workload. Like many managers, you may have several projects to look after at a time; some are likely to be more or less urgent than others. Spending time on a daily or weekly basis prioritising jobs for yourself and your team should help you to ensure that the more urgent jobs are carried out first and that valuable time is not wasted on less urgent work which could be delegated or routinised.

Other time-wasting occurrences include:

- dealing with unwanted visitors
- telephone interruptions
- social chit-chat
- travelling
- dealing with other people's problems

It is worth spending a little time thinking about each of these and how such wasted time can be prevented. For example, if you have a secretary, or assistant, perhaps he or she could deal with visitors and filter your telephone calls. Identify specific times when you cannot be disturbed by telephone or by unplanned visitors. Use travelling time to and from work productively; in other cases, write or telephone instead of calling in person or see if someone else can go. Encourage people to think about solutions to their problems before coming to you for help in deciding what they should do.

Delegation

Delegation does not, and should not, be used as an excuse to pass on the more boring work to your staff. This will not motivate them nor play a part in their development. Nor will it really help you to save time because it is unlikely to be done well and in the end you may have to do it yourself anyway. It is better to see delegation as an opportunity for staff development, giving other people more challenging and worthwhile tasks, which will save you considerably more time than delegating boring and repetitive ones.

One of the reasons managers do not delegate effectively is because they are perfectionists and expect their staff to achieve unnecessarily high standards, as the two examples below, from managers on a training course, illustrate.

> I used to spend several hours doing unnecessary paperwork, although I have a production assistant who is supposed to do it. I realized that the reason I was doing it myself was because I expected the production assistant to achieve a perfect result every time. When I thought about it, a satisfactory result would have been good enough and the occasional failure wouldn't have been a disaster. By changing my thinking, I was able to delegate more tasks to the assistant and use my own time more effectively.

> I find it difficult to delegate, mainly because I don't want my staff to feel I delegate too much. I feel this could be seen as a weakness and also as suggesting that I do not trust them to do the job as well as I do. This means when I do delegate, I am constantly checking on them to ensure the work is up to standard – my standard. At my appraisal, my manager discussed this failure of mine to delegate and suggested I saw it as helping my staff to understand their jobs better. Now I delegate the daily completion of work figures and the production of a weekly plan to my team and it is amazing to see how much better they understand how well – or poorly – they are performing.

Managing your workload

We have touched on workload planning in relation to setting priorities and, of course, it is also related to effective delegation. Managers often spend considerable time in planning and allocating the work of their staff, and very little on organising their own workload. However overwork and work-related stress are two of the major problems faced by today's managers, while the work–life balance is an issue which has steadily risen up managers' agendas in recent years.

In an extreme example of this, Japan's biggest advertising agency was forced to pay more than £1 million to the family of a man who committed suicide after working for 17 months without a day off. Ichiro Oshima often worked late – at times until dawn – with only two or three hours' sleep before returning to his desk by 9 am. Death from overwork, or 'karoshi', has long been a sensitive issue in Japan, where workaholic tendencies are widespread because of pressures to be loyal to the corporate 'family' (Joyce 2000).

Rosemary Stewart (1982) developed a way of looking at a manager's job in terms of its demands and constraints and the degree of choice, or control, which the individual can exercise. 'Demands', according to Stewart, are tasks you must do. Demands can come from your superiors and your peers, from people outside the organisation in the form of requests for information or action, from the system in the form of reports or budgets you are required to submit, from your staff who may need guidance or appraisal and, finally, from yourself – the work you feel you must do because of your personal standards or habits. You may be able to reduce some of these demands, but not others.

'Constraints' limit what you can do. These may include resource limitations, legal regulations, union agreements, technological or physical limitations, organisational policies and procedures and people's attitudes towards you, and expectations about your role as a manager. Such limitations are often difficult to change.

The area of 'choice' shown in figure 2.1 is the extent to which the manager can choose what is done (or not done) and how it is done; there are also usually elements of choice in when the work is done, by whom (delegation) and to what standard.

In figure 2.1, Job A has heavy demands and between these demands and the constraints within which it is performed, there is little area for choice. Job B, on the

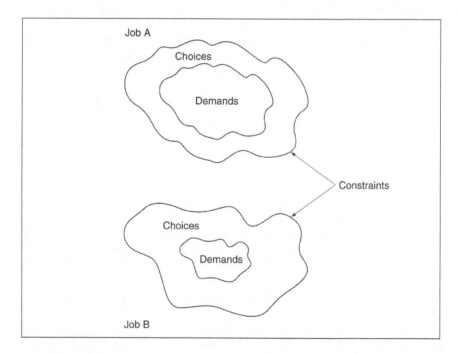

Figure 2.1 Looking at the demands and constraints of managers' jobs.

other hand, leaves the manager with considerable area of choice between the demands of the job and the constraints within which it is performed. The manager who holds Job A really needs to look at the demands of the job; there are too many of them, some of which may be unrealistic. Maybe he or she needs more staff so that some of the demands can be passed on to others; or perhaps a discussion with the line manager might reduce some of the demands which are being imposed from above.

A part of managing your workload is achieving an appropriate work–life balance, and this is far from easy for many managers. British workers have notoriously long working hours compared with their European counterparts, and managers work amongst the longest hours within the workforce. Obviously a key to the work–life balance is consideration of and time spent with your family, but a balance is not just about this. It is very desirable to have interests outside work whether these are hobbies, sport or membership of organisations, for example. These can help you to maintain your health (particularly where they involve taking exercise) and can also help you to manage stress.

Applying these ideas to your own experience

Try describing your job in terms of demands, constraints and choice. If the demands made on you are too heavy, how might these be reduced? Using your area of choice, can you plan your workload more effectively?

Managing stress

Workload is an important source of stress both for managers and for those who work for them. A recent report (CIPD 2013) based on a survey of over 2,000 employees revealed that nearly a quarter regularly felt under too much pressure at work; half said that their workload had increased over the past 12 months and nearly half said that they had experienced an increase in stress over the same period. The authors pointed out that for managers the problem was worse, since they had to manage both their own work pressures and support their teams in managing theirs. Change can be another source of stress and can itself add to the problems of workload pressure.

We all vary in the amount of pressure we can cope with before we start to feel stressed, and the symptoms of stress can take many forms. Common symptoms include becoming more easily upset, whether this takes the form of tearfulness, being aggressive or changes in eating or sleeping patterns, for example. All these can also, however, be symptoms of other conditions too. Here is a longer list of some of the wide range of possible reactions to stress:

- difficulty sleeping
- being over-sensitive

- increased blood pressure
- difficulty concentrating
- feeling tired, overworked or bored
- increased irritability
- increased dependency on cigarettes, alcohol or tranquillisers
- anxiety
- depression
- mood swings
- eating too much or too little
- headaches
- stomach problems.

If you feel that you are suffering from workplace stress you may find that managing your time and your workload as already discussed will help you to address this. Coping with stress can also be helped by engaging in activities completely unrelated to work, which can help you to relax and feel refreshed. If none of these approaches works, you could consider seeking help or advice. Your organisation may have an employee support programme, perhaps including a counselling service, which can help you. Other possible sources of help include your doctor or external counselling services (your doctor may be able to advise or provide a referral).

You will find more detailed guidance on identifying and managing stress on the website of the Health and Safety Executive, which is an independent body set up to reduce work-related injury and death (www.hse.gov.uk). You will also find guidance in Chapter 8 about your own responsibilities as a manager in relation to workplace stress and the ways you can support your own staff.

Making decisions

There are, according to the American social scientist Herbert Simon, two main kinds of decisions which anyone is called upon to make. There are 'programmed' decisions, which can be made for problems or events that have occurred before, such as processing a customer's order, determining an employee's holiday entitlement or carrying out any routine job. In addition, there are 'non-programmed' decisions, which have to be made where there is no cut-and-dried method for handling the problem, either because it has not occurred before or because it is particularly difficult or important. To help with the uncertainties of non-programmed decision-making, Simon developed a model of rational thinking which involved three stages – intelligence, design and choice (figure 2.2).

The three stages could be broken down into a series of smaller steps. At the intelligence stage, the problem needs to be defined and clarified so that everyone is clear about what the problem actually is. Once the problem has been defined, then criteria need to be drawn up so that any solution can be evaluated against these. In the design stage, possible solutions should be generated and, in the choice stage, these possible solutions should be evaluated against the criteria and the best option selected.

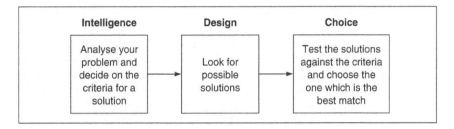

Figure 2.2 A rational decision-making model.

Applying these ideas to your own experience

Think about a problem you have at work and which you have to address. Try applying the rational decision-making model to this problem.

Managing meetings

Meetings inevitably play an important role in any manager's working life and it is worth learning how to make good use of the time you spend in them, whether you are chairing or attending as a participant. This section is really about formal meetings, but some of the points in it are relevant to informal meetings too. For example, it always makes sense to be clear about the purpose of a meeting, however informal, and to make a note of any actions agreed there.

In a formal meeting participants are advised about the purpose of the meeting by the agenda, which sets out what will be covered and in what order and is normally circulated in advance. It is the chair's responsibility to ensure that the agenda is correct, that the order makes sense and that enough time is allocated for each item. It may also be necessary to send information out with the agenda and even to have pre-meeting discussions if you need individual participants to make a particular contribution – to make a presentation for example.

As chair, you can set the tone for a productive meeting by starting promptly and, where necessary, by making sure all attendees introduce themselves. This is particularly important if you are meeting online, as it is very easy for individuals to feel excluded if they are not able to see the other members of the meeting. It is usual to start a formal meeting by noting apologies, checking whether everyone present agrees that the minutes of the previous meeting (if there was one) are accurate, and picking up any issue arising from the minutes, such as queries about actions agreed there.

When you are chairing a meeting your task is to ensure that every agenda item is discussed as fully as it needs to be, that all interested parties have the opportunity to contribute and that the meeting does not run over its allocated time. You may find that this means stopping, firmly but politely, anyone who wants to dominate the meeting, and also helping those who find it difficult to speak to do so. You can do this simply by asking individuals if they have any comment to make, for example.

One of the hardest parts of managing a meeting is keeping to time. Busy meetings can easily drag on, and you must stop speakers who drift from the point. You can also help the discussion to stay focused by summarising the key points already made and, where necessary, reminding the meeting of the issues to be addressed. Your aim should be to keep your meetings as short as is compatible with a full discussion of the issues – and your attendees will thank you for it.

You will need a note-taker to record the main points of the discussion and it is good practice to identify and record who is responsible for any actions agreed. This enables you to check easily that all actions have been followed up. It will be your job as chair to ensure that the minutes are accurate, even if they are not written up by you.

As a participant in a meeting you will always find it helpful to be clear about its purpose, so it is worth spending time reading the agenda and thinking about any facts you need to gather. Decisions may be made which affect you or your team so you will want to be prepared to make your case and to present the relevant information clearly and precisely. If you are in disagreement with others (as commonly happens in meetings), try to understand their perspective and be constructive about the way forward. You should also make sure you are clear what has been decided and where necessary inform others about the implications for them of what has been decided.

Communicating

Managers need to communicate and communication is a two-way process. Depending on the type of communication, it can involve giving, receiving or seeking information. Even the casual greeting, 'Hello, how are you?' is, effectively, seeking information about the other person's state of health. The common reply, 'Fine – how about you?' is both giving and seeking information on the speaker's part, whilst the listener is receiving information.

We communicate with a wide range of people in our working lives, as figure 2.3 shows, and this can be called our 'communication network'.

We can categorise the ways in which we communicate into the spoken word and the written word, although this neglects communicating pictorially or graphically. We can also take into account the non-verbal aspects of communicating.

Communicating through the spoken word includes face-to-face communication between individuals and groups, presentations and speeches, telephone conversations and communicating face to face online. Written communication can be on paper in the form of letters, memos, reports, newsletters, articles, books and so on and via electronic means such as email, computer-mediated conferencing and social media. Non-verbal communication can include the tone of voice, accent, facial expression, gestures, body language and personal choice of clothes and decoration.

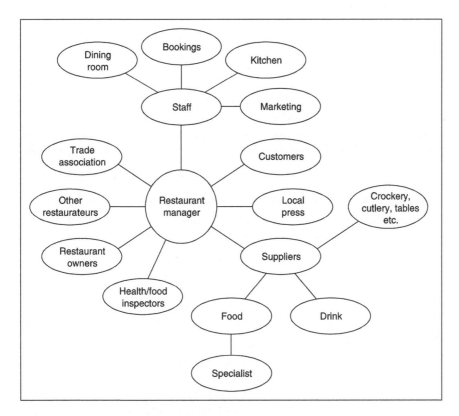

Figure 2.3 A restaurant manager's network.

But communication is not a simple process and too often people can misunderstand what others have said or written. It is not just what you communicate but how you do it. The use of complex, long-winded language can create problems in understanding, as can using an inappropriate method of communicating. For example, complicated directions are usually communicated more effectively through a map than by word of mouth – providing the map is accurate! Jargon can cause difficulties for people who are not familiar with it, as can acronyms. 'Take the hot batch down to TCR right away' could be incomprehensible to anyone not familiar with the terms and initials.

Communication is also about what you are trying to achieve. Managers usually have three objectives in communicating: getting employees to understand and accept what the manager proposes should be done; obtaining the commitment of the employees to these proposals; and helping the employees to appreciate the contribution that they will be making to the success of the proposals and how this will benefit them. It follows that communicating is more than merely telling people something but should also include a capacity for foreseeing and appreciating their likely response. What you say therefore requires thinking through before you say it. A golden rule in communicating effectively is continually to reflect back on what has been said, checking that your understanding matches that of the speaker, and to check, when you are speaking, that the listener shares your understanding of what you have said.

Communicating is also about informing people about issues that they might reasonably expect to know about. People will only feel part of a team and appreciated if they are kept informed about developments. Briefings, newsletters or other means of informing people should also provide some means by which they can also express opinions. Most people will not do so, but will nevertheless welcome the opportunity.

Applying these ideas to your own experience

Try drawing up your own communication network. You can make this more complex and realistic by drawing communication links between others on the network – for example, in figure 2.3, the restaurant owner would probably communicate with other owners. Now make a list of the different ways in which you communicate with other people.

Active listening

Part of your job as a manager is likely to involve listening to people – listening to their problems, their successes and worries, their reports on progress, their reasons for not progressing, their grievances and ideas. Listening is a skill and 'active listening' is a particular skill; instead of passively absorbing what is being said, it entails trying to understand what the speaker is saying and helping them to clarify for both of you what they mean. It is very easy to listen without hearing what is being said, which is why this section is titled 'active listening'.

Another very important part of the value of active listening lies in its contribution to your knowledge of what is happening in your unit, and being an effective manager means knowing what is happening around you. It is often not what is said that is important, but how it is said. Unless you can understand the nuances of what people are trying to tell you, you may miss the reality of the situation. Gossip, jokes and casual comments are part of the key to understanding the informal dynamics of your unit and the wider organisation.

The skills of active listening take time and practice to acquire. As a manager, you have many opportunities for the second of these. Next time someone comes into your office with a problem, try the following:

- Either give them your full attention at that moment or arrange a time when you can give them all your attention.
- Don't take the words at face value; encourage the person to expand on what they are saying.

- Watch the non-verbal communication; is the person more or less worried than he or she appears – are there signs outside the words themselves which indicate anything?
- Check your understanding of what is being said; reflect in your own words what the speaker seems to be saying – perhaps you have misunderstood them.
- Try to convey 'I respect you as a person and feel you are worth listening to' through all your words and actions.
- Encourage the person to try to articulate possible solutions to the problem.

As a manager, it is important to recognise and to be sensitive to the personal challenges your staff may face in the workplace and to be supportive when necessary. Active listening, or listening in a way that really helps you to understand the other person's perspective, can help; and it can also help you to understand better the impact you are having on others in the things you say and do.

Often, as a manager, your communications with staff will really be about helping them to work out for themselves how to deal with issues and problems. Coaching and mentoring can both be used in this way and are core skills for effective managers. They draw on similar skills, one of the most important of which is active listening. Both are very much focused on helping people to learn and you will read more about them in Chapter 5.

Applying these ideas to your own experience

Can you think of a time when a colleague or manager has listened actively to you and helped you to think through a problem or an issue? If you cannot think of an example in the workplace, can you think of an example of someone outside work, perhaps a friend or member of your family, who has done so? If so, can you identify lessons you can learn from this interaction about how to listen well to others?

Developing yourself

The constant pace of change in organisational life means that the skills you will need as a manager will change. Your role will change too, as the organisation around you changes and expectations of you change with it. This means that to remain effective you will need to focus on constantly improving your skills and developing new skills. This continuous learning and development is often referred to as continuous professional development (CPD). You will read too in Chapter 10 about the importance of a commitment to lifelong learning, which goes beyond skill development in the workplace and can lead to powerful personal growth.

Good self-development requires critical self-awareness. It requires an ability to identify your own strengths and areas for development, and it requires the commitment to follow through. It is important to be able to take the initiative yourself, and in all probability go beyond the range of learning and development offered by your employer if you are to meet your own wider career needs. It also means being proactive in looking for opportunities to develop your skills. This could be through training courses (perhaps sponsored by your employer) or studying for a qualification. It could equally be through seeking other opportunities to develop new skills. You could, for example, take on a new responsibility, or you might shadow a colleague or manager in their role – either of these might be negotiated with your manager at your performance appraisal or performance review. Or you might seek mentoring or coaching from a more experienced manager. (See Chapter 5 for more on both approaches to learning.)

Used systematically, these approaches should steadily improve your skills and experience. To learn continuously, however, you really need to go one step further and make a practice of drawing learning from your experiences in the workplace. This means developing the skill of reflecting on your experiences and drawing learning from those reflections to inform your practice in the future. This ability to learn and to keep on learning, and to draw learning from your experiences, whether successful or not, can be a key factor in being effective at work and in career success.

You may also find it helps to seek feedback from those who know you well about how you are performing. This doesn't mean asking for praise or criticism, but asking what specifically went well and what went less well. Sometimes you will get praise or criticism without seeking it and when this happens it can be worth trying to work out what exactly produced the positive or negative reaction so that you know what to do to repeat the first and avoid repeating the second. It is also always worth remembering that feedback, praise and criticism may be fair or unfair – so when you have carefully considered what you can learn from any of these you are entitled to disregard or forget them!

In the example below, you will see how Sam used both reflection and feedback to improve his skills:

Sam's presentation to his team had not gone well. They had to wait while he struggled to get the projector to work and then it took a while to find the slides he wanted to use. Because he was flustered he then forgot to make some of the points he had intended to make and he realised that his team were not all listening – some seemed to be checking their phones or sending emails. Worse, Sam's own manager was at the team meeting and didn't seem too impressed.

Reflecting back afterwards, Sam resolved that next time he would make sure he was better prepared and had the presentation ready to go before the meeting started. He also decided to ask for feedback from Aidan, a member of his team whom he trusted. Aiden told him that it wasn't always easy to follow Sam's points because he was so often looking down at his notes and seemed unconfident. Sam decide to make sure that the next time he would practise his presentation so he wouldn't have to rely so much on his notes and would find it easier to look at his team while he was speaking to them. Unsurprisingly, his next presentation went a lot better.

You may work for an organisation which encourages continuous learning and development. This may be set out in a learning and development or management development policy and you may find that your appraisal or performance review requires you to show how you are managing your learning. However, even where this not the case you are likely to reap benefits from this approach, both in managing your workload and in managing your career.

Applying these ideas to your own experience

Think about a recent experience at work which you would have liked to have gone better. Can you think of ways you could have improved it? Is there someone you trust at work, perhaps a colleague or your manager, who might be able to give helpful feedback but how to improve further?

Managing your career

Your career, like your skills, needs to be managed actively, not just left to develop by chance or at the behest of an employer. This involves being able to look backwards as well as forwards, and to be able to learn from what has happened to date. The concept of career is becoming more diffuse, and very few managers can now expect a job for life. You should ask yourself what your objectives are, and identify your career 'anchors', which reflect your values and priorities. Schein (1978) identified eight different categories of career anchor:

- technical/functional, where the anchor is achieving specific skills
- entrepreneurial, where the anchor is developing a business
- general managerial competence, where the anchor is general management
- service/dedication, where the anchor is commitment to a moral goal
- autonomy/independence, where the anchor is being your own master, even in employment
- pure challenge, where the anchor is being challenged by a job
- security/stability, where the anchor is a safe and stable job
- lifestyle, where the anchor is the balance of external interests with the career.

Planning your own career and self-development involves acquiring information about jobs inside your own organisation and possibilities outside it. It means matching your strengths to the requirements of other jobs and reducing your weaknesses through training and skill acquisition. It requires a lot of self-investigation, complete honesty and determination.

Managing your manager

Your line manager will be one of those who makes demands on you in your job and will be the person responsible for appraising you and discussing your performance with you. He or she is likely to be asked for a reference if you are seeking promotion or a new job and can represent your interests and those of your team to senior management. All this means that your manager can often play an important role in helping you to develop your career – and equally can block your progress. This means that the soft skills you need in managing your own team are equally important in helping you to build a good and constructive relationship with your line manager.

A good line manager, with whom you have built a strong relationship, should help you to make the best use of your strengths and to overcome your weaknesses. He or she may take your part in inter-departmental negotiations and should support you, deal with you fairly and honestly, delegate and communicate effectively and give you opportunities to be involved in decision-making, particularly when the decisions affect you and your area of responsibility.

Unfortunately, you can rarely choose your line manager and some will be much more skilled and competent than others. If you are unlucky enough to work for a manager who does not appear interested in you, perhaps sees you as a threat, does not involve you in decisions or tell you what is happening, doesn't delegate and so on, it will be doubly important to manage this relationship carefully. Here are some suggestions for approaching this:

Don't:

*   get into shouting matches or arguments
*   put up with discrimination on unfair grounds or harassment
*   provide opportunities for resentment through poor time-keeping, inadequate work performance, excessive absenteeism etc.

Do:

*   if necessary ensure all your dealings with your manager are recorded in writing
*   consider consulting your manager's manager
*   consider discussing the situation with your colleagues to find out if they are also experiencing problems
*   take any instances of unfair discrimination or harassment to a higher authority in the organisation
*   if necessary consider using your organisation's grievance procedure to express your dissatisfaction.

Applying these ideas to your own experience

Spend some time thinking about how well your relationship with your line manager works. If it is not as good as it could be, can you think of ways you could improve it?

Activities

1. At the end of each working day, allow yourself 10 minutes in which to list and prioritise the tasks for the next day. Allocate one hour of the next day to the boring and difficult tasks (the first hour of the day for example) and tackle them then.
2. How could you reduce your workload and use your time more productively by delegating some of it to your subordinates?
3. Try to get hold of the job description and person specification of a post which you aspire to in your organisation. Evaluate your personal strengths and weaknesses against the requirements of the job and, if possible, get someone else at work who knows you well to give you feedback on your self-assessment. What can you learn from this exercise about your self-development needs?

References

CIPD, (2013) *Employee Outlook: Focus on Employee Well-being.* London, Chartered Institute of Personnel and Development.

Goleman D., (1996) *Emotional Intelligence: Why It can Matter More Than IQ.* London, Bloomsbury.

Goleman D., (2001) 'Get Happy, Carefully', *Harvard Business Review*, 79(11), 49–51.

Joyce C., (2000) 'Death from overwork costs £1 m', *The Telegraph*, 24 June. Available on-line at www.telegraph.co.uk/news/worldnews/asia/japan/1344775/Death-from-overwork-costs-1m.html [accessed 6 May 2014].

Schein E., (1978) *Career Dynamics: Matching Individual and Organizational Needs*, Reading, Mass., Addison-Wesley.

Stewart R., (1982) *Choices for the Manager.* New York, McGraw Hill.

3 The recruitment cycle

Introduction

Every employee has a life cycle of activities in a particular organisation: recruitment, selection, induction, retention and departure. How to manage these five stages is obviously a significant issue for the organisation and also for the front-line manager who has primary contact with the employee. This chapter is concerned with how each stage can be most effectively managed, starting with defining future staff requirements and planning the recruitment, selection and induction of staff, particularly in your own area of responsibility.

These are in some respects the most important of your tasks as a manager, since by far the biggest component of the successful management of people is having the right people to pursue the organisation's objectives. In recruiting staff you will focus on attracting the best potential candidates, whilst selection can be defined as choosing the best person for the job from among candidates who come from within the organisation or from outside. It involves setting up fair selection processes which, as far as possible, are designed to predict how an individual will behave at work and whether he or she can perform a specific range of tasks at least satisfactorily.

Many organisations will go to considerable lengths to make themselves attractive to potential applicants by the way they present themselves to them. This is particularly important when the skills you need are not easily found and makes the conduct of the recruitment and selection process critically important. Poorly treated candidates may complain about their treatment (using social media for example) and this can make it harder for you to attract staff in the future.

Once you have succeeded in appointing good candidates you will want to keep them. An effective induction process will help them to settle quickly into their new roles and will help you to encourage them to stay in the organisation (retention) and to ensure that they are not unnecessarily disaffected and encouraged to leave the organisation. When the individual does leave the organisation, for whatever reason, it is important to try to understand why this has happened. This makes it possible to identify and address avoidable reasons for employee departures.

In this chapter, we will be examining the following topics:

*   determining human resource requirements
*   carrying out a job analysis
*   drawing up a job description and person specification
*   methods of recruiting candidates
*   the selection process
*   shortlisting candidates
*   interviewing candidates
*   induction
*   retention
*   departure.

Determining human resource requirements

The decisions you make about recruiting and selecting staff in your own area of responsibility will ideally be set in the context of overall organisational personnel requirements. If you work in a large organisation there may well be a specialist planning function, which estimates the likely future need for human resources and works out how this is likely to be met. As a first line manager you may be asked to contribute to this planning function by making an estimate of your staffing needs.

In any case, it makes sense as a manager to think about the resources currently available to your team and those you will need in the future. This means considering what you expect to have to achieve in your area of responsibility and the ways in which your objectives can be achieved. This includes the numbers and type of staff likely to be needed in both the short- and long-term future and the likely availability of staff to meet these requirements. The first stage, however, in developing a plan for your area of responsibility involves analysing the skills and knowledge already available to you amongst the people already working for you – sometimes called a skills audit. In this way, you can begin to identify skill deficiencies and plan to remedy these through recruitment. In making these judgements, however, it makes sense to consider developing the skills of your existing staff to meet predicted requirements. Providing development opportunities can often improve levels of motivation and commitment and it is much cheaper to keep people than it is to recruit them. You will read more about the importance of retaining staff later in this chapter.

Sometimes it is also possible to cover a vacancy by reorganising the way work is carried out or by restructuring existing posts within the organisation. If done carefully, so that existing staff do not feel overloaded or disadvantaged, this can create an opportunity to use existing resources more effectively and may even create an opportunity to make existing roles more interesting and satisfying.

Applying these ideas to your own experience

What methods does your organisation use to plan for future staffing levels? Does it provide a clear indication of the type and numbers of staff the organisation will need in the future?

Carrying out a job analysis

Once you have decided that a genuine vacancy does exist, you will need to start to define the job so that you can provide a description of what is required for the purposes of recruitment and selection. We will refer to this as a job description. You will also need to provide a person specification, which sets out the skills experience and personal attributes required of the successful candidate for the role.

The first step is to find out what the job you intend to advertise will entail. Your objectives in carrying out a job analysis are fourfold:

- First, what is the purpose of the job? Is it necessary? Is it fulfilling its purpose?
- Second, could it be combined with other jobs to make it more fulfilling or could some parts be reallocated to make better use of the skills of other people in the department?
- Third, could a full-time job be shared between two people working part time? Could all or part of the job be carried out in the jobholder's home? Could more flexible working hours be introduced? This would enable you to widen your recruitment to include people who, for a variety of reasons, could not undertake either a full-time job or travel to and from home.
- Fourth, what have you learned about the role from analysing it?

Once you are confident that you have a good sense of what the job entails you will need to think about whether there are ways in which the job is likely to change in the near future. Will the next jobholder require different skills if the job is to change or grow? For example, is your organisation planning to move into markets outside the UK and are you likely to need people who can speak languages other than English or who are willing to be mobile?

Applying these ideas to your own experience

What patterns of work does your employer use? Does your organisation operate any job share schemes, opportunities for homeworking or flexitime? If not, could these be introduced?

Drawing up a job description and person specification

A good job description is a vital part of recruitment. Acas, the Advisory, Conciliation and Arbitration Service, suggests that it should include the following:

1. The main purpose of the job
    Your job analysis should have teased this out and you should aim to describe the purpose of the job in one sentence. For example: the purpose of this job is to supervise the work of secretarial and clerical staff in the department in order to provide high quality secretarial support to the senior management team.
2. The main tasks of the job
    Here, again, the job analysis should have identified these but you need to make them as clear as possible. Use verbs such as 'filing . . .', 'designing . . .', 'planning . . .' etc, which actively and specifically describe what the job involves.
3. The scope of the job
    This means giving an indication of the size of the job and the responsibilities it involves. These include, for example, the number of people for whom the jobholder would be responsible, the budget he/she would control or how the job itself relates to the overall work of the department or organisation.

(Acas 2014)

Once you have completed a satisfactory job description, you should draw up a description of the type of person who you feel would best perform the job. This is a person specification and will typically cover the following:

*   skills
*   experience
*   qualifications
*   education
*   personal attributes.

(IRS, quoted in Taylor 2014: 123)

In each case, you should specify 'essential' and 'desirable' qualities. Those which are categorised as 'essential' are so necessary that without them, the job could not be performed either effectively or efficiently. 'Desirable' qualities should be seen as additional assets, which would enhance effective performance of the job. It is important that you identify essential qualities accurately. If you specify as essential attributes which actually are not essential and which are more easily met by one gender rather than another, one age group rather than another, or one racial, ethnic, national or religious group rather than another, you will risk discriminating unlawfully (this is known as indirect discrimination and you will read more about it in Chapter 9). Remember too that employers are required by law to make 'reasonable' adjustments to their policies, premises and/or working practices in order to make a job accessible to a disabled person (again, see Chapter 9 for more on this).

Everything you include in the person specification should relate closely to your job description and should be capable of being described and measured so that you are able to make an informed and accurate decision about the best candidate for the job.

Further information for candidates

Potential employees will want to know more about the job than normally appears in the job description or the person specification, so you will need to provide additional and complementary further information for candidates. This should include any information about the job not included in the job description, such as its place in the organisation and the terms and conditions of employment. It should also include information about the organisation as a whole, such as its size, achievements and future plans. It is good practice to include the name and telephone number of someone in the organisation whom candidates can contact if they want to ask questions about the job and also information about how the selection process will be carried out.

Applicants should always be provided with the job description, the person specification and the further information for candidates.

Methods of recruiting candidates

The purpose of the recruitment process is to attract candidates to apply for the job or jobs being advertised. The aim is to generate a pool of applicants from which the successful candidate or candidates can be chosen; if the task of recruitment is carried out poorly and the candidate pool is weak, the selection process will be compromised. In other words, without effective recruitment of candidates there cannot be a successful selection process.

An important first step is to decide whether you need to recruit candidates from outside the organisation to take over a vacant job. If you have carried out an audit of the people in your area of responsibility, you should have a good idea of the skills, knowledge, experience and attitudes of your existing staff and it may make more sense to promote someone internally or to move someone sideways as part of their career development.

Many organisations have a policy of giving preference to internal candidates, at least in certain circumstances, such as where internal reorganisation has created a pool of surplus candidates who would otherwise be vulnerable to redundancy. In any case, there are obvious motivational benefits in ensuring that internal candidates have a good chance of achieving promotion, and operating an internal labour market policy also helps to cut the costs of recruiting and inducting new staff.

On the other hand, it can make sense to keep a balance between internal and external recruitment. Sometimes it is important to bring in new ideas and skills from outside the organisation. Also, if you rarely recruit external candidates you are less likely to have a diverse workforce, with the variety of perspectives this can offer.

Advertising externally

A great deal of external recruitment advertising has now moved online, particularly in areas such as graduate recruitment; social media such as Twitter, Facebook and LinkedIn are increasingly popular. However, there is still a place for advertising in print media such as newspapers and specialist magazines, although this can be expensive. Other approaches to recruitment include using recruitment agencies, headhunters and job centres to source applicants. In all these case the choice about where to advertise will be informed by judgements about where the best candidates for the job being advertised will be reached and about the cost-effectiveness of the method being used. Cost in this case is measured against the value to the organisation of getting exactly the right person for the role.

This targeted advertising may be complemented by other methods of ensuring a supply of external candidates. For example, organisations may cultivate links with educational institutions, such as schools, colleges and universities, which are a good supply of job applicants. Other approaches include holding open days or using general advertising to encourage potential candidates to consider a particular career or industry. Some organisations promote themselves as a brand, using marketing techniques. The Chartered Institute of Personnel and Development (CIPD) defines an employer brand as 'a set of attributes and qualities – often intangible – that makes an organisation distinctive, promises a particular kind of employment experience, and appeals to those people who will thrive and perform best in its culture' (CIPD 2007: 3).

However you choose to advertise, you should ensure that you do not, intentionally or otherwise, discriminate on grounds which are unfair and irrelevant to the job being advertised. All candidates and potential candidates for employment are protected by law from discrimination on the grounds of race or ethnic origin, religion, disability, age, gender and sexual orientation, although the Equality Act 2010 does allow employers to discriminate where they can show an occupational requirement to do so. However, there are very few cases where this can be justified and you should be careful to seek advice before you rely on this as a defence against claims of discrimination. You will read more about the law relating to unfair discrimination in Chapter 9.

Online recruitment

Most large organisations advertise for vacancies on their own website and this can be combined with one or more complementary recruitment activities, which may include other forms of online recruitment. This can mean advertising on an online employment website such as Monster.com or one of the rather smaller, specialised sites such as jobs.ac.uk (specialising in higher education vacancies). Employers provide details of jobs to these sites, which potential candidates can access; in some cases the sites alert candidates who subscribe to them of suitable vacancies.

The advantage for employers is in the very low cost and the speed with which they can get a job vacancy advertised on the internet, which can be accessed by people outside the UK as well as inside. It is sometimes argued that online recruitment is not suitable for certain types of job, where computer literacy is unimportant and also that this may deter candidates without access to the internet from applying. On the other hand, where the work involves being able to use a computer, online recruitment seems appropriate and its use is spreading quickly. Many organisations will not now accept applications except online and this trend seems likely to increase.

Social media

Social media offer opportunities for online recruitment, which are relatively new but growing fast in popularity. Like other online recruitment tools they offer significantly lower costs and speed of access to candidates (Broughton and others 2013). They also offer potential for targeting individuals with particular profiles, and where they can be used in lieu of recruiters and headhunters there can be very large savings.

Recruitment agencies and headhunters

There are now many well known companies that specialise in providing staff, reflecting the increasing numbers of organisations which have externalised their recruitment activities. However, they can be quite expensive, charging a percentage of the first year's salary. Within the same category (and often the same companies) are those which provide temporary or contract staff.

Headhunters, or as they often prefer to call themselves, recruitment consultants, are normally only used for recruitment at very senior levels. They can produce a shortlist after trawling likely applicants and sometimes carrying out a preliminary interview. Their advantage is that they can approach individuals who are unlikely to be reading advertisements, and who may have no immediate intention of leaving their existing employer. Although not cheap, they can be cost-effective if they find the right person.

The application form

You are also going to have to consider in what form you want applications to be made. Your organisation may have a standard application form, in which case you should have a look at it and decide whether it meets your needs or whether it needs to be adapted or redesigned. Any application form should be designed to give the maximum information about the candidate that is relevant to the requirements of the job. This can include educational, technical and/or professional qualifications essential for performance of the job, previous job history and relevant experience and any special requirements, such as the ability to speak a particular language or the need to hold a current driving licence. You may also ask for a CV or a letter of application instead of, or in addition to, a completed application form: look at the requirements of the job and decide which form(s) of application would be most useful when it comes to making an initial selection.

The application form should not normally require information that is not relevant to the role. However, information about sex, race, ethnicity or national origin, age, sexual orientation, religious belief or disability may be collected separately in a form which plays no part in the selection process but which enables your organisation to monitor its effectiveness in avoiding discrimination on any of these grounds.

Your application form should, however, ask whether applicants need you to make any adjustments to your selection process because of disability. You should also ask whether the candidate has a legal right to work in the UK. It is the employer's responsibility to make sure anyone taken on has a legal right to work in the UK and in the area of work to which you are recruiting and you will need to ask for documentary evidence of this before you employ any member of staff. If you do not have an HR specialist to advise you, you will find guidance on the employer's responsibilities and acceptable documentation on the government website (Home Office, 2008).

Applying these ideas to your own experience

Which methods of recruitment does your organisation use? Should you be thinking about widening the recruitment net by investigating other methods?

The selection process

Once you have attracted the right candidates, you move to the task of selecting the right person for the job from those who have applied for it. This means setting up fair selection processes which, as far as possible, predict how an individual will behave at work and whether he or she can perform effectively in the job. You will have made the choice about which selection process to use at the recruitment stage, so that details could be included in the further particulars.

The most common method of selection is the face-to-face interview and, since you are very likely to take part in one of these, we will look at the interview process in some detail in the next section. Alternative or complementary methods of selection include psychological tests and the use of assessment centres. Psychological tests, which include tests of ability and personality tests, can be valuable providing the test is relevant to the job which has to be performed and that the tester has been trained in its use. Assessment centres are not places but processes, involving candidates being assessed on various work-related tests by a range of assessors. They are considered to be valid, reliable and fair as a means of selecting people as long as they are well designed and the assessors are skilled and carefully trained.

In addition, there are a number of less well known methods. One of these is bio data (short for biographical data), which uses information from a candidate's past to make judgements about suitability for a role. This appears to have high predictive ability but is not widely used in the UK, perhaps for cost reasons.

Psychological testing

The psychological tests used in selection fall into two main categories: ability testing and personality testing. In both cases they measure differences between individuals which are relevant to the workplace. They must be supported by a body of evidence which confirms that they do measure what they claim to measure and that these measurements are repeatable over time – in other words that they are valid and reliable. Only occupational psychologists are qualified to train people in applying and analysing these tests and it makes sense to seek professional advice before choosing any test for selection purposes. An important factor to take into account is that psychological tests can have inbuilt cultural biases and should only be used if the test providers can confirm that they will not produce results which are unfairly biased.

Ability tests usually focus on mental abilities such as verbal, numerical and spatial abilities and specific tests have been developed for certain types of work such as computer programming, for example. Tests can be used to identify high potential candidates and results may also be benchmarked against those of individuals working in the role the candidate aspires to, at the level of seniority to which he or she aspires.

Personality tests measure aspects of personality and may, for example, measure the degree to which a person can be categorised as extrovert or introvert, as stable or neurotic, as dependent or independent. They must be interpreted by someone trained in their use and can help to identify areas to be probed at interview. It is worth remembering that in the case of widely used tests candidates may have seen them before and may even have practised answering them.

Assessment centres

Assessment centres incorporate exercises derived from detailed job analysis and include exercises which test candidates' ability to perform in work-related exercises and in which they are evaluated by a number of assessors, often drawn from senior staff from the workplace in question. These tests are costly and since they are normally designed for the specific workplace they are usually used only when significant numbers of candidates are being assessed. The exercises may focus on:

- prioritising tasks in an in-tray
- group problem-solving
- consensus decision-making
- role play simulations.

The resulting data are then evaluated and scores are derived for each candidate. They may be complemented by psychological testing and interviews so a range of assessment methods can be drawn on to achieve a final result. These methods are now being widely used, particularly in large organisations for promotion as well as recruitment of external candidates.

Selection for promotion

Much of what has been written in this chapter also applies to selection for promotion. Although a job description and person specification may already exist, these may need to be updated. Internal vacancies should be advertised if they are open to all and, of course, great care should always be taken to avoid unfair discrimination.

The form and conduct of the selection process should be as rigorous as that for any job vacancy in the organisation. In particular, there need to be arrangements whereby unsuccessful candidates are given full feedback on their performance and, if necessary, counselling about their future career prospects.

Shortlisting candidates

Whichever selection method you choose, the first step in the selection process will be to choose a shortlist of the applicants you want to consider in more detail. This means looking carefully at each application and measuring it against the 'essential' and 'desirable' qualities you identified in your person specification. Only those who meet the essential requirements listed in your person specification should be shortlisted. You may also need to look at the desirable characteristics to reduce your list further. You may need to prioritise your list of desirable qualities before making a final decision – are some more valuable than others?

You should keep a careful note of the reasons why each individual candidate was rejected, giving a clear reason why the person cannot fulfil the requirements of this particular job (this should relate to the characteristics set out in your person specification). Some organisations now insist on the completion of a form at this stage, which gives individual reasons for not shortlisting all applicants, so that feedback can be given to those who ask for it. If you do not give adequate reasons for not shortlisting people for further selection, you run the risk of being accused – rightly or wrongly – of discrimination on grounds not related to the job advertised.

Once you have reduced your list of applicants to a manageable size, you may also want to call up references. Treat these with caution, however, as their predictive validity is very limited.

Applying these ideas to your own experience

What selection methods are used in your organisation?

Interviewing candidates

Selection interviews have had a bad press; they have been widely criticised as being both unreliable and invalid as predictors of future performance. Critics have claimed that, for example:

- interviewers may make up their minds about a candidate within the first five minutes of the interview and – consciously or unconsciously – spend the rest of the interview trying to justify their judgement
- interviewers' judgements of candidates can be affected by their appearance, speech, gender and race either positively or negatively; they may favour those whom they perceive to be like themselves
- it is difficult for interviewers to concentrate at the same level over a prolonged period; thus if you are interviewing several candidates on the same day, they may not receive equal amounts of your attention.

Despite these concerns, interviews remain the most widely used method of selection for two reasons: first, they are relatively inexpensive, and second, many people feel a strong need to meet and talk to someone before appointing them. Moreover, many of the potential problems can be avoided if interviewers are properly trained and if the interviews are carefully planned. So, if you decide that an interview is going to be part of your selection process, you will need to make it as robust a selection method as possible. There are four main factors which can affect the success or failure of a selection interview:

- the amount of preparation before the interview
- the conduct and form of the interview
- the kinds of questions the interviewer asks
- the quality of the final decision-making process
- preparation.

A large part of the necessary preparation for the interview should already have been carried out by drawing up a person specification and matching applications against this. However, you will need to read each application form carefully to identify for each candidate any areas you need to probe further. There may also be information available on how candidates have performed in other selection methods, such as those outlined later in this chapter – information on their achievements in assessment centres, for example, or results of psychometric testing. All relevant information on each candidate should be collected and analysed before interviews take place (figure 3.1).

Your purpose at the interview is to obtain, as objectively as possible, as much relevant and accurate information about the candidate as you can. You may also need to think about the kinds of questions candidates are likely to ask. These might include questions about salary scales, career progression, opportunities for staff training and development, holiday entitlement and so on. As the interviewer you will need to be prepared, as far as possible, to give the answers.

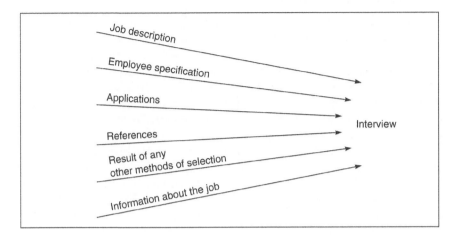

Figure 3.1 Information you need before the interview.

Form and conduct of the interview

Your main decision in this area is about who should be involved in the actual interviews. One-to-one interviews can be less threatening to potential candidates than panel interviews, but they have disadvantages in that only one person makes the decision and the interviewer has no opportunity to listen to candidates' answers to other interviewers' questions. Large panels (of more than four or five) allow less time for individual questioning and demand more time when it comes to making selection decisions; they are can also feel very threatening to candidates and are more expensive.

Whatever form of interview you decide to use, if it involves other people they will need to have all the essential information about the candidate beforehand and they should meet to discuss how they will handle the main areas of questioning. They should also agree on the conduct of the interview. If there is to be a panel, it will need a chair who will be responsible for welcoming and introducing each candidate, for ensuring that all the major points have been covered by the other members of the panel and for summarising at the end of the interview. The chair will also be responsible for ensuring that the final decision is communicated to the successful and unsuccessful candidates.

The way you treat candidates will affect the way they see you as a potential employer and it makes sense to send even unsuccessful candidates away feeling well disposed and able to contemplate applying for a future post. Candidates who feel poorly treated will not speak well of you to others. For example, applicants for jobs as van drivers at B&Q were upset at being asked to dance and pull faces before their interviews. While B&Q said this was a light-hearted and optional exercise, the story was reported nationally and attracted criticism for the organisation (BBC 2007).

Questions asked by the interviewer

Your preparation and discussion with other people involved in the interview process should have identified the areas you need to question for each candidate. It is sometimes argued that all candidates should be asked exactly the same questions, in the interests of consistency and fairness. We believe, however, that whilst it makes sense to start with a common set of questions for each candidate, interviewers do need to be able to depart from these to probe areas of particular concern. Thus, if a candidate is clearly under-qualified, for example, or indeed over-qualified, you will need to address this in questioning.

Many candidates are nervous when they come for an interview and unless you put them at their ease, you will not get the best out of them. At the start of the interview it helps to spend a few moments on general and unthreatening issues such as how the candidate got there or the weather. Thereafter, you can help them in the way you phrase your questions. You can make a choice, depending on what kind of answer you are looking for, between any of the following:

- Open questions – which are designed to draw the candidate out such as, 'How did you go about setting up a networking system in your last job?' or 'What did you learn from this training course you went on last year?' or 'What appeals to you about this job?'
- Closed questions – which are used to clarify a point of fact and often only require a short or single word answer. For example, 'Did you head up the team?' or 'Was that your own idea?' or 'Did you or your employer decide to do that?'
- Hypothetical questions – which can be used to find out how a candidate might respond in certain situations such as 'If we offered you this job, how would you go about improving communications between departments?' or 'If you had a budget of £100,000 for promoting a new product, how would you spend it?'
- Probing questions – which are necessary if you feel a candidate has not given you a full answer and you want to find out more. They can be used immediately after a candidate has referred to something you would like to know more about by saying 'Exactly what happened next ...?' or you can return to an earlier point by saying, for example, 'I'd like to go back to something you said earlier about not enjoying your work on the project team. Could you tell me why you didn't enjoy it?'

You should try to avoid asking several questions at the same time, such as:

> Tell me how you got your present job, what attracted you to it and which parts of it you like best and which parts you like least. Do you prefer it to the job you had before that?

This leaves the candidate confused as to which part of the question should be answered first and both the candidate and the interviewer are likely to forget parts of the original question.

There are also questions you should not ask. These include questions of a personal nature that are not relevant to the job and/or could be described as unfairly discriminatory. For example:

- 'How old are you?'
- 'Are you married?'
- 'What religious holidays do you observe?'
- What arrangements do you have for childcare?'

It also makes sense to avoid questions which:

- are likely to take the candidate a long time to answer, such as 'Tell me about your previous jobs'
- are designed to give you the answer you want rather than the real answer, such as 'Wouldn't it have been more efficient if you had brought in a specialist to deal with that part of the job?' or 'You don't like working on your own, do you?'
- probe sensitive or emotional issues unless these are truly relevant to the job.

A widely used interviewing technique uses examples from the candidate's own past experience to focus on the skills needed for another job. This is known as competency-based or behavioural interviewing. For example, if you had analysed a job which you felt required quick decision-making, the ability to work under pressure and the need for diplomatic handling of problems, you might ask questions like the following:

- 'Give me an example of a time when you had to make a decision quickly'
- 'Can you describe any job you have held where you were faced with problems and pressures which tested your ability to cope?'
- 'Can you give me an example of a time when you had to conform to a policy with which you did not agree?'

Some candidates, often through nervousness, will talk endlessly and pointlessly if given the chance. You will need to bring them back to the point courteously, perhaps by rephrasing the question or moving on to another area. It is perfectly acceptable for you and other interviewers to take notes during the interview; in fact it is preferable if you are interviewing more than one person on the same day. It is a good idea to explain to the candidates that you intend to do this as an aid to decision-making, but try not to make your note-taking obvious, particularly when probing sensitive areas.

When you have asked all the questions you feel are necessary, you should give each candidate an opportunity to ask questions of you and other interviewers. Do not be surprised if they do not have any questions – you may have answered their concerns satisfactorily in the information you have already provided.

You should be careful not to make promises to candidates which cannot be fulfilled, such as assurances about training and promotion if they take the job. Apart from being morally wrong to promise something which, later, cannot be provided, employees will be resentful if they feel they took the job under false pretences. Sometimes, interviewers are so keen to appoint a particularly outstanding candidate that they make offers, often in good faith, to encourage the person to join the organisation; later, when the offers do not materialise, the dissatisfied employee may feel bitter enough to make a formal complaint.

Finally, when closing the interview, thank the candidates for coming and let them know when and how they can expect to learn the outcome.

Making a decision

Despite all your efforts at obtaining the best range of candidates, briefing other interviewers and controlling the interview itself, it is likely that when it comes to making a choice out of, say, six candidates, that different interviewers will have made different choices. When this happens, the differences between candidates need to be discussed with reference to the essential and desirable qualities set out in your person specification so that the decision-making process is transparent and justifiable. It makes sense to be systematic about this because you must be able to explain to unsuccessful candidates the reasons why they were not selected and, in any case, your organisation may require these reasons to be given in writing for their own records.

Once a decision has been reached, the successful candidate should be offered the job and those who were unsuccessful need to be told. Again, bear in mind that these unsuccessful candidates might be successful in future and give as much feedback as possible as to why each failed to get the job. Remember, too, that until the candidate has formally accepted a job offer in writing, the candidate might change his or her mind.

Applying these ideas to your own experience

Think back to a selection interview in which you were involved and compare it to the guidance you have just read. What can you learn from this about how you would want to behave as an interviewer?

Induction

The first few weeks, or even days, of a worker's experience of a job can have a lasting impact on their longer-term view of it. People are at their most vulnerable at this point before they really appreciate the requirements of the job or get to know their colleagues and it is quite common in some industries for employees to leave in their first months in a new role. Good induction can help to encourage workers to want to stay and you, as the line manager of new members of staff, have an important role to play in this. You can directly influence their early experiences of the workplace and the relationships they form with you can be an important factor in how they feel about their new employment.

Induction might be said to consist of three rather separate sets of activities: an introduction to the organisation and the role; socialisation or the process of adjusting to the organisation; and any more formal training and development necessary for the job. The introduction to the organisation may well be partly at the organisational level, with various contractual, payments, pension and similar dimensions of becoming an employee; with this there may also be something like an organisation video to explain the wider organisation to incomers, and probably various explanatory documents. But there will also be an introduction to immediate colleagues and people in other sub-units with whom there may be a work relationship. And most of all there will be a welcoming meeting with the immediate manager to clarify responsibilities and to reconcile expectations on both sides.

This introduction is followed by an equally important next stage of socialisation, in which the incomer begins to understand his or her colleagues as individuals and personalities rather than just names, and begins to understand the informal norms, values and processes of the unit and the organisation. This latter is often forgotten in the induction programme, and is best taken into account by appointing a mentor or at least a 'buddy' to whom the new employee can turn for advice and who can take a proactive approach to assisting in the socialisation process. The third stage is the initial training and development the employee needs on joining the organisation. This will in large part be about the demands of the specific job, but should also relate the job to other aspects of the organisation.

Induction is not always given to temporary or short-term staff in the belief that they will not care much about the organisation as a whole and that they are just there to do the job. Nevertheless, many organisations rely heavily on part-time or temporary staff and use them on a regular basis. A good induction process will help these staff to feel their role in the organisation is valued and can help them to make an effective contribution to it.

Applying these ideas to your own experience

What induction do you and your organisation provide for new staff? Do you think it is good enough, and if not, how might it be improved?

Retention

Recruiting new staff and helping them to settle into their new role is both time-consuming and expensive, and it makes obvious sense to ensure that once they are in post they will be content to stay for some time. Some of the factors which may encourage employees to leave (such as higher pay or shorter travel time for example) will be outside your control, and in any case some staff turnover is expected and even desirable. It is expensive, however, and employees should not be leaving because they feel unfairly treated or are uncomfortable in their team or with the organisational culture for example. None of these is compatible with an organisation where employees feel valued and willing to give of their best, and they are all areas you can control as a front-line manager.

Taylor (2014) points out that poor line management is the major driver of unwanted turnover and this again emphasises the importance of the role of the front-line manager. Conversely, good people management practices, as we have outlined them throughout this book, will help to ensure that employees are satisfied and unlikely to seek new employment. It is worth remembering that pay may be a significant factor but is not necessarily a critical one, and that learning and development and career development can also be very important to some employees.

Departure

Employees may leave the organisation for a number of reasons, some of which can be controlled by the organisation (or manager) and some of which cannot. They include:

- dissatisfaction with the organisation and/or the behaviour of particular managers
- more attractive opportunities elsewhere
- retirement, illness or family relocation
- dismissal or redundancy.

When employees do leave the organisation it makes sense to try to understand why this has happened so that the causes, if avoidable, can be addressed. Exit interviews, which ask employees for their reasons for leaving, are widely used, although the evidence they provide may not be reliable. You may also find clues in satisfaction surveys, if your organisation has these. Although usually anonymous and not specific to teams or departments, these surveys can alert you to issues which may be causing your staff dissatisfaction and give you a chance to address them before they lead to resignations.

Once the decision to leave is made, there are various procedures to be gone through such as the need for a resignation letter, tax issues and perhaps agreement about future references. It is usually in the interests of both parties to maintain good relations during this period, partly for the reputations of both sides and partly because there is a period of notice to be worked out. A farewell event is a final expression of goodwill on both sides, and treating a departing employee well can send a positive message to remaining employees about the employer's regard for them.

Managing employees in a way which motivates them and encourages them to be committed and engaged is likely to encourage them to stay with the organisation. We will look more closely at motivating and engaging staff in the next chapter.

Activities

1. Choose the job of someone for whom you have responsibility and conduct a job analysis.
2. Draw up a job description, based on the job analysis you have just conducted, and then a person specification based on the job description.
3. Imagine that you have been asked to take part in or lead a selection interview for this post and note down the essential questions you would ask candidates.
4. Develop an induction plan for the successful candidate.

References

Acas, (2010) *Managing Retention and Employee Turnover*. Advisory booklet. London, Acas.

Acas, (2014) *Recruitment and Induction*. Advisory booklet. London, Acas.

BBC, (2007) *B&Q 'dance routines' criticised*. Available on-line at http://news.bbc.co.uk/1/hi/business/6226157.stm [accessed 31 July 2014].

Broughton A., Foley B., Ledermaier S. and Cox A., (2013) *The Use of Social Media in the Recruitment Process*. London, Acas. Available on-line at www.acas.org.uk/research papers [accessed 12 May 2014].

CIPD, (2007) *Employer Branding: A No-Nonsense Approach*. London, Chartered Institute of Personnel and Development.

Home Office Border and Immigration Agency, (2008) *Prevention of Illegal Working*. Available on-line at www.gov.uk/government/uploads/system/uploads/attachment_data/file/311831/antidiscriminationcode2008.pdf [accessed 27 May 2014].

Taylor S., (2014) *Resourcing and Talent Management*, 6th edition. London, Chartered Institute of Personnel and Development.

4 Getting the best out of people

Introduction

There is a dramatic difference between a workplace where workers simply do what they are asked to do and one where they are fully engaged and willing to make an extra effort to get a good result. This attitude to work can be an important source of competitive advantage and there are a number of factors that can contribute to it and support it. This chapter is about what you as a front-line manager can do to encourage the members of your team to be fully motivated and committed to their work; and help you to understand why some people appear to be committed to their jobs and others less so.

A great deal of research has been done in recent years to find out what organisational practices and management practices can improve motivation and you will read more about these in this chapter. You will also read about the practices that have been recognised for some time as being important in influencing individual motivation and which remain relevant today. These include recognising the different needs individuals have and the different benefits they value, and the job itself and the way in which it is designed. Most important of all, however, is understanding the behaviours you can use as a line manager to improve motivation and performance in your team.

Of course, it is not possible to engage and motivate everyone and this reinforces the importance of the recruitment and selection issues we considered in the last chapter in ensuring that the right people are recruited in the first place. It also remains important to manage performance effectively through performance management systems and you will read more about this in Chapter 7.

You will also need to take into account the varying skills and needs of those you manage. In the last section of this chapter you will read about managing and getting the most out of a diverse workforce.

In this chapter we will be considering:

*   employee engagement and why it matters
*   your role as a front-line manager
*   motivation and job satisfaction

- job design
- alternative methods of organising work
- managing a diverse workforce.

Employee engagement and why it matters

Engaged workers are committed to doing their job well and demonstrate this by making an extra effort to achieve a good result. This willingness to do more than required (sometimes referred to as discretionary effort) can make a considerable difference to an organisation's performance and a great deal of research has been done in recent years to identify what organisations and managers can do to achieve this result. It is important to note that engagement means more than just being satisfied: Storey and others (2009) point out that satisfaction relates to how much workers like their jobs, but that it is quite possible to like a job without working hard at it. Engagement can be defined as 'a set of positive attitudes and behaviours enabling high performance of a kind which is in tune with the organisation's mission' (Open University 2014: 1).

Employee engagement is seen as so important in producing high performance in the workplace that the government commissioned a review led by David McLeod to explore it and its potential benefits both for organisations and for those who work in them. The subsequent report observed that if the workforce is to be engaged, four things need to be in place:

celebrating success - audit

- leadership that enables employees to see how their work is contributing to the organisation's purpose
- managers who motivate and support their staff
- opportunities for employees to express their views, even when they are challenging, and to be listened to and feel that their opinion matters (this is sometimes known as employee voice)
- behaviours in the organisation, which are consistent with and reflect the values that the organisation claims to espouse.

McLeod reported that, whilst many companies report high levels of engagement in their workforce, in others levels are low, with many managers still relying on instructions to get work done and still assuming that workers are only motivated by pay. Emphasising the importance of managers' role in getting staff to give their best the report comments:

> If it is how the workforce performs that determines whether companies and organisations succeed, then whether or not the workforce is positively encouraged to perform at its best should be a prime consideration for every leader and manager and be placed at the heart of business strategy.
>
> (McLeod and Clarke 2009: 3)

Your role as a front-line manager

As a front-line manager you have a critical role in influencing the attitudes and motivation of your staff. However carefully your organisation designs its HR policies, the way they are experienced will depend on how they are delivered in practice by line managers. Purcell and Hutchinson (2007) noted that the negative effects of poorly designed HR policies can be moderated by effective line managers; and the converse is also true.

Acas suggest that front-line managers' performance in each of these areas will influence the way employees feel about their employers and their performance in their work. Examples of suggested behaviours are shown in table 4.1.

In the next sections of this chapter you will read more about motivating the employees for whom you are responsible and helping them to feel fulfilled and satisfied in their work.

Motivation and job satisfaction

Motivation is both highly individual and complex and there is a difference between what motivates people to perform above average and what leads to below-average performance. Managers too vary in their attitude towards those they manage and the assumptions they make about them – and these attitudes and assumptions can themselves have an important impact on staff motivation.

Table 4.1 Manager behaviours which make a positive impact

Area of work	Behaviours which make a positive impact
Performance management	Make a connection between personal and organisational goals Reward employees for their performance and innovative ideas Motivate staff through positive feedback
Work–life balance	Set a good example by providing lunch, rest breaks and annual leave Retain valuable members of staff by being flexible about working patterns Develop empathy by recognising personal needs
Learning and development	Coach staff to improve their skills and improve trust
Communication and involvement	Make policies more effective by involving employees and their representatives Front-line managers have a clear role in communicating with their staff
Openness and conflict management	Investigate problems so you really know what is going on Develop trust and team working
Employee representation	Work closely with trade union and/or employee representatives in consultative committees and working groups and on an informal basis

Source: Adapted from Acas (2014)

One well known difference between managers in the way they approach their staff was set out by Professor Douglas McGregor (1960). Based on his observations of management during his years as a senior administrator in an American college, he suggested that managers make either theory X or theory Y assumptions about the way others behave. Theory X assumptions include the following:

- that the average human being inherently dislikes work and will avoid it if possible
- that, because of this, subordinates must be coerced, controlled, directed or threatened with punishment to get them to put in adequate effort at work
- that the average person prefers to be directed, wishes to avoid responsibility, has relatively little ambition and wants security above all else.

Perhaps you know of managers who have all or some of these assumptions about the people who work for them; perhaps you yourself think about some other people in this way. Theory X has had its followers for a long time and can certainly be used for explaining some kinds of behaviour in organisations. More recent research on people at work, however, supports McGregor's set of theory Y assumptions, which include the following:

- that most people do not inherently dislike work and that, according to the conditions, it may be a source of either satisfaction or punishment
- that people will generally exercise self-direction and self-control in pursuit of objectives to which they are committed
- that most people learn, under proper conditions, not only to accept but to seek responsibility
- that most people are not being used by organisations to their full potential
- that, in order to obtain commitment from employees, rewards should fulfil an individual's self-actualisation needs (we will be looking at self-actualisation later in this chapter).

Whether managers choose either the set of assumptions associated with theory X or with theory Y, there will be a tendency throughout the organisation for people to respond to the way they are managed. Therefore, if employees feel that they are not being trusted, for example, they may behave in a less trustworthy way.

The theory Y explanation of the way we may think about other people at work included a belief about the kinds of rewards that people value. Frederick Taylor, an engineer and the exponent of the idea of 'scientific management', observed: 'What the workforce want from their employers beyond anything else is high wages and what employers want from their workforce most of all is low labour costs of manufacture ... the existence or absence of these two elements forms the best index of either good or bad management' (Taylor 1947). This attitude is not compatible, as you have already seen, with ideas about engaging employees so they are encouraged to be fully committed to their work. However, it remains true that wages and the level of pay for a job are important elements of a reward system.

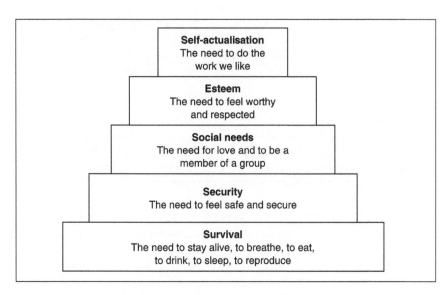

Figure 4.1 Maslow's hierarchy of needs.

Motivation based on satisfying individual needs

An alternative explanation of human behaviour was put forward by the psychologist Maslow, who believed there were five levels of need which the individual sought to satisfy. The lowest of these included the basic physiological needs for food, drink and shelter; once these were satisfied, individuals needed to protect themselves against danger, threat and deprivation – safety needs. Thereafter, the levels of need rose through social needs, the need for self-esteem and status (ego needs) to the need for self-actualisation (figure 4.1). Maslow explained self-actualisation as follows:

> A musician must make music, an artist must paint, a poet must write, if he is to be ultimately happy. What a man can be, he must be. This need we may call self-actualisation. ... It refers to the desire for self-fulfilment, namely the tendency for him to become actualised in what he is potentially ... the desire to become more and more what one is, to become everything that one is capable of becoming.
>
> (Maslow 1943: 382)

Later researchers have questioned the hierarchical nature of Maslow's explanation but share in his belief that people work for different reasons and that these reasons may include financial rewards, although only as part of an overall reward system.

Satisfiers and dissatisfiers

Frederick Herzberg's research into the motivation of accountants and engineers revealed a number of factors that affected the way in which people felt about their work (Herzberg and others 1959). These included:

- achievement
- recognition from others
- the work itself
- responsibility
- opportunities for advancement
- company policy and administration
- supervision
- salary
- interpersonal relations
- working conditions.

Those factors that made people feel satisfied with their job and motivated them to work included high levels of achievement, recognition, opportunities for advancement and responsibility. The content of the work itself was also very important. Factors that affected employees adversely and which led them to feel dissatisfied with the work they were doing included company policy and administration, supervision, salary, interpersonal relations and working conditions; if all or any of these were considered by individuals to be of a low standard, employees felt dissatisfied with what they were doing.

The important lesson here is that if the factors classified by Herzberg as 'dissatisfiers' (or 'hygiene factors') can be improved and the level of the 'satisfiers' or motivating factors increased, performance should improve. However, merely improving the 'dissatisfiers' will not result in any long-term increase in an individual's motivation to work, although it may produce short-term results and increase job satisfaction.

Having identified some general factors that can increase or decrease job satisfaction, it has to be recognised that each individual is likely to value these factors according to their own needs. For example, people with young children are likely to value the provision of childcare at work and flexible working hours more highly than people who do not have these responsibilities. Some companies have concentrated on improving job satisfaction for employees with young children. But there are others whose dependants may be elderly or infirm, and people whose partners may be ill, unemployed or in prison. There is a significant minority of people with no partners and who may or may not have dependants – all of these are unlikely to benefit from childcare schemes. To some an expensive company car may bring satisfaction, whilst others might value more free time to spend in leisure pursuits. In some cases, training incentives or a flexible retirement decade will increase job satisfaction and commitment to the organisation.

Rewards do not always need to be tangible, such as bonus payments, promotion or other benefits. These are extrinsic rewards because they depend on someone else.

Intrinsic rewards, however, are those feelings that result directly from performance of a task – rewards such as a sense of achievement, of having done a good job, of having done the job better than it was done before, of having done something worthwhile. Of course, intrinsic outcomes are not always rewarding; you can experience feelings of fatigue, frustration or disappointment as a result of performing a job less well than you had hoped. You will read more about rewards and their role in performance management in Chapter 7.

Applying these ideas to your own experience

Can you think of ways to increase the motivation of your staff, for example by increasing job 'satisfiers' and decreasing 'dissatisfiers'?

Job design

Changing the design of jobs can increase job satisfaction and benefit individuals, management and the organisation as a whole. Well-designed jobs are characterised by the amount of skill variety, task identity, task significance, autonomy and feedback they involve. Job satisfaction can be increased through methods such as job rotation, job enrichment and the creation of autonomous working groups.

Much of the early work on designing jobs was undertaken in the 1970s by companies such as Saab, United Biscuits and ICI, who were pioneers in experimenting with job redesign and work reorganisation. Although these organisations aimed at improving job satisfaction, their 'hidden agenda' was to improve productivity. However, as you have seen, increased job satisfaction does not always result in increased performance and a number of other factors need to be addressed if workers are to be fully engaged and 'go the extra mile'.

Increasing job satisfaction, however, can produce a number of advantages to the organisation, to the manager and to the individual employee, as set out in figure 4.2.

Organisational benefits

When employees are satisfied with the work they are doing and with the work environment, they are likely to identify more closely with the employing organisation and it is likely to be easier to get commitment and engagement from a satisfied workforce. There is less likelihood of industrial unrest.

Management benefits

Managers may or may not find better performance from subordinates who are satisfied with the work they are doing (you have already seen that being satisfied with a job does not in itself mean that you will work harder at it). However, disruptive symptoms of dissatisfaction, such as absenteeism and illness, are less likely

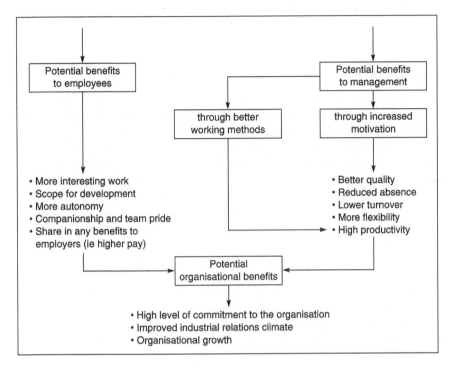

Figure 4.2 Improving job design and work organisation to meet individual needs.

Source: The Effective Manager, Book 4, Open University, 1996

to be present and employees are likely to be more willing and able to perform a range of jobs if their individual skills and abilities are fully developed.

Individual benefits

If a person with particular skills and abilities finds his or her job suited to those qualities, the work they are doing will be more interesting and, thus, less likely to produce stress. Repetitive and boring work is, in fact, highly stressful, particularly if it involves little opportunity for moving about. The job should have some scope for development of the individual so that he or she can see opportunities for improvement and advancement. With more control over the work, the individual has an increased sense of autonomy and freedom as to the way in which it can be carried out.

However, these are potential benefits and you should not expect, just by redesigning a job, that all of them will naturally occur. There are, as usual, a number of other factors to be considered, such as the expectations and abilities of individuals, the kind of organisation in which you work and its reward systems and, finally, the kind of work that has to be performed. Although we will be looking at alternative ways of performing jobs later in this chapter, most of us work under certain constraints, not least the expectations and demands of our bosses, customers or clients.

Characteristics of a well-designed job

The main work on job design was carried out in the 1970s by Hackman and Oldham (1976), who developed a set of five core job dimensions or job characteristics. These were the essential ingredients of a well-designed job and, in an ideal situation, all five should be present. If they were, Hackman and Oldham argued, the individual would feel the job was meaningful, would have a sense of personal responsibility for the outcomes of the job and would, through feedback on performance, be personally strengthened and motivated to improve. The overall result would be high quality work performance, high internal work motivation and satisfaction for the individual and reduced absenteeism and staff turnover.

Hackman and Oldham's core job characteristics consisted of:

- skill variety
- task identity
- task significance
- autonomy
- feedback.

Skill variety

This characteristic refers to the extent to which a job requires a variety of activities so that the individual can use a number of different skills and talents. Not everyone enjoys jobs with a high degree of variety, however – some people prefer a more routinised job with which they feel 'safe' and able to cope. Others prefer as wide a variety as possible, providing they have the skills to undertake these or can be provided with the necessary training and development.

Task identity

Some jobs are less satisfying than others because not only do they use few of the jobholder's skills and abilities, but the job itself forms only a small part of a whole. The person doing the job cannot see its outcome in concrete terms. Assembly-line work, where an operator is only responsible for a small task, such as welding together two pieces of metal or screwing several nuts on to passing bolts, has little task identity unless the person can see their part in the final outcome. Experiments with changing from an assembly line production method to one where each person puts together a whole or a major part of the finished product have been very successful in increasing job satisfaction – and output. Individuals become responsible for overall quality, as well as the manual tasks involved.

Task significance

How important is your job to the organisation? Or the job of one of those who work for you? How good do they feel about the jobs they are doing? Task significance relates to the extent to which the job has a substantial impact on the lives and work of other people either within the work environment or outside it. People who work for voluntary organisations such as charities, for example, and are unwaged may be highly motivated because they feel that the work they are doing has a significant impact on others who are less fortunate than themselves. Hackman and Oldham cite the example of people who tighten nuts on aircraft brake assemblies; they are likely to see their work as more meaningful in terms of the overall safety of the aeroplane, its crew and passengers than someone who fills small boxes with paper clips, even though the skill levels are similar.

The significance of the job will, again, depend on the individual's personal values, which is why some people choose to work for a charitable organisation, or teach children with learning difficulties or take up nursing, whilst others elect to program computers, drive long-distance lorries or sell designer clothes. In each case, it is the extent to which the person is satisfied by the task that he or she is doing that is important.

Autonomy

Autonomy refers to the amount of freedom and discretion the individual can exercise over the job. A job with high autonomy is likely to engender a sense of responsibility – which Herzberg (1968) identified as being one of the main elements affecting job satisfaction – providing that person wants and can cope with this. Some people prefer jobs with a low level of responsibility where they are told what to do and work to a strict schedule; this can be true, for example, when people have a highly complex and demanding life outside work, leaving them little energy or desire to take on additional responsibility in their jobs. However, mistaken assumptions about the degree of responsibility individuals wish to take on can lead to considerable dissatisfaction.

Anna noticed that her new secretary, who had seemed very keen on the job at first, was performing less and less well as time went on. She was making mistakes in simple letters, had been abrupt on the telephone with several of the senior consultants, took long lunch breaks and had been off sick for a day or two at a time on several occasions. On taking her to task about all this, Anna discovered that the woman was bored with the job. 'There are lots of things I could do which you do yourself,' she complained, 'for example, you don't need to dictate every letter – just tell me what you want to say and I'll compose it. And I can organise your diary for you so that you don't book two meetings at the same time – I get the blame for that anyway. I can set up your meetings as well, and contact the other people.'

Feedback

People need to know whether they are performing their jobs satisfactorily; they need praise for doing things well and they need help and advice if they are not performing up to standard. This may – and usually should – involve you in giving individual feedback to your staff, but other performance measures such as quality checks, formal appraisal and performance reviews can be used for this purpose. It helps to give feedback regularly and promptly if you can so that it has the maximum impact and benefit.

Although Hackman and Oldham's job characteristics were developed nearly 40 years ago, they are still recognised as being of value today. Unfortunately, not enough jobs contain all the characteristics and there is nearly always room for improvement.

Designing or redesigning the jobs of your staff

Very few of us get the chance to design jobs from scratch; sometimes you may be lucky enough to be involved in drawing up job descriptions or specifications for new jobs created as a result of growth or the introduction of new technology. And, of course, you can use the opportunity created by recruitment to redefine an existing job.

Designing the job itself is one part of the process; the other is matching the right person to the right job so that the degree of skill variety, task identity and task significance matches the needs and abilities of the individual. There are, however, a number of ways in which some of the characteristics identified by Hackman and Oldham can be improved, including:

* job rotation (increasing skill variety)
* job enrichment (increasing responsibility and thus task identity, task significance and autonomy)
* autonomous working groups (increasing autonomy).

Job rotation

Job rotation is one way of increasing skill variety as well as being a method of introducing new employees to a wider area than their own job. It is a form of internal job transfer and can reduce the boredom and monotony associated with repetitive, low-level jobs. Its benefits, however, are limited in making any lasting contribution to job satisfaction.

Job enrichment

Job enrichment (sometimes called job enhancement) can be very effective in increasing satisfaction providing it is aimed specifically at increasing the level of responsibility of the individual. It should not be confused with 'job enlargement', which too often means simply giving the employee more work of the same type.

In five years, Bausch and Lomb's factory in Waterford changed from a traditional assembly line with standard job evaluation and grading to a new, cellular system based on teams. Before the change, members of the design team toured the factory, interviewing employees. They asked everyone whether they liked their job, how it could be improved and, specifically, whether they would like a wider range of tasks and more responsibility. The answer was an overwhelming 'Yes'.

Autonomous working groups

Increased responsibility and autonomy can also be provided by team working where the team is responsible for work allocation and organisation. The construction industry, where work is sub-contracted to teams of workers, is a good example of this. These working groups can also provide opportunities for increased skill variety and opportunities for more flexible working and individual development. Additionally, they provide social companionship and a sense of pride in the team's work. Not all teams are effective, however, and conflict may arise between team members, particularly if there is individual competition for different tasks; there is also the need for team leaders to be trained in the skills of leadership and supervision if they are to take over the duties of work organisation.

Applying these ideas to your own experience

Are autonomous working groups used in your area of responsibility or in the organisation more widely? If not, can you see how you might introduce them to improve job satisfaction?

Alternative methods of organising work

Since the traditional 'job for life' concept has virtually disappeared and the widespread introduction of new technology has had a major impact on job design, there is an increasing opportunity to survey normal working practices and see whether these could be changed.

Flexible working hours, job sharing, home working and adaptation of work methods for people with disabilities are some of the more enterprising ways of work organisation. They are not without their problems nor, in some cases, without high initial costs, but they can all bring benefits if well managed. In examining these possibilities, as indeed with job design more generally, consideration must be given to health and safety at work, which is discussed in more detail in Chapter 9.

Flexible working hours

Many organisations already operate flexible working arrangements and all employees have, since July 2014, the right to request flexible working arrangements.

Flexibility in working arrangements is attractive to employees and can contribute significantly to job satisfaction. The organisation can benefit from lower absenteeism, better time-keeping, reduced staff turnover, higher work commitment and improved performance; employees see the advantages of more leisure time, less time spent commuting at peak times, increased responsibility and the ability to schedule work and personal life to the individual's satisfaction.

Flexible working hours can range from a daily, fixed-but-flexible starting and finishing time to the working day to a system of annualised hours over a full year. In the first case, employees may work any eight consecutive hours, for example, between 7.30 am and 6.30 pm. This has the added advantage in providing maximum cover for essential operations such as telephone enquiries or emergencies over a longer period than the typical 9–5 working day. Or they may work a given number of hours during a working week or fortnight, some of which is designated as 'core time' (when staff are required to be at their place of work) and the rest as 'flexible time'. This flexible time might account, for example, for four hours of any working day; in agreement with the manager, the employee can select which particular four hours he or she will work for the rest of each day.

However, annualised hours systems involve a great deal of management time to set up, agree and implement. One of its undoubted benefits is the ability to roster employees to work more and longer hours during peak times and fewer, shorter hours during slack periods.

Compressed working week

This arrangement allows employees to work longer than normal hours for part of a week and have the rest of the time free. It is another variation of flexible working hours but can result in increased fatigue at work, concern and resistance from unions and increases the chance of employees taking on 'second jobs' during their free time, potentially reducing commitment and increasing fatigue.

Job sharing

In a job-sharing arrangement, two part-time employees split one full-time job; the salary and hours of work are usually split equally but there is also room for unequal shares. This can benefit people with childcare or other dependant commitments, people who tire easily or have physical limitations, people who want to indulge in part-time study and older people who want to phase in their retirement. Providing the two job sharers communicate fully with each other, this arrangement can work well, but continuity is essential.

Career-break schemes

Although not defined as an alternative working method, organisations that make provisions for employees to take career breaks whilst retaining their right to return to work at a later date usually benefit from such schemes. They are normally aimed at women or men who want to take time at home to be with young children but they can also be used for employees who want time off to study full time or to experience working practice elsewhere. With the need to recruit and retain more women in the workforce, career-break schemes make good sense to enterprising employers.

Working from home

Although considerable potential savings in rents, heat, lighting and travel could be made if more people worked from home, this is still regarded with suspicion by many employers. There is a feeling of lack of control – but this may simply be a lack of trust in subordinates. Advances in technology and reductions in its cost make it a sensible option to consider.

Jobs that involve a great deal of computer-based work can readily be done from home. Employers provide mobile phones, answering machines, pagers and laptop computers needed for home-based employees to keep in touch with colleagues and clients. People whose work involves a considerable amount of travelling, such as social workers and sales staff, can also use their home as a base rather than take up office space that is left empty most of the time.

Not everyone wants to work from or at home, however. Many people enjoy the social life they find at work and not all home environments are suitable for working in. The loss of social interaction, informal meetings and conversations with colleagues and knowing what is going on can lower an employee's interest in and commitment to the organisation.

Applying these ideas to your own experience

How many of the flexible working practices described in this section are used by those working in your area of responsibility? Can you see opportunities to use any that are not currently in use?

Managing a diverse workforce

Encouraging those who work for you to give their best means treating them as individuals and recognising and valuing the differences between them and the unique contribution each makes in the workplace. It also means taking their different needs into account. This is particularly important because the workforce you manage is likely to be diverse.

There are many different aspects of diversity, including gender, race or ethnic origin, religious belief, age, language, disability and sexual orientation. The Workplace Employment Relations Study of 2011 (van Woonroy 2013) indicated, for example, that 51 per cent of employees were women, that 30 per cent were over 50, and that 9 per cent were non-white. There are many other dimensions of diversity; different shift patterns, different job functions, different grades of work can also constitute differences which require the management of diversity; and people have different personalities, which may need different management styles if they are to be engaged and motivated.

Differences can have considerable advantages. In particular, diverse groups and teams can reflect the real world much more fully than a homogeneous group that can easily lose sight of wider issues. They are also likely to be less inward-looking and produce a wider range of perspectives. However, they can also present challenges. If you are part of a new team, brought together as part of a project, you will need time to get to know one another. Another – and increasingly common – possibility is working in a multicultural team with people of different nationalities, which brings its own challenges. Members of the team may have quite different assumptions and expectations, for example, about working practices.

It is quite common in the UK for managers to work beyond their contracted hours; in fact, it is often seen as a sign of dedication and commitment. Scandinavian managers, on the other hand, are used to finishing work at somewhere between 4.30 pm and 5 pm and consider people who stay on beyond that time as inefficient or incompetent. In the USA and the UK, team members usually refer to each other by their first names. This is not the case in Germany, and some Scandinavians expect to be called by their last name only. Even assumptions about leadership and authority can differ quite widely amongst European Member States. Team leaders in the Netherlands, Scandinavia and the UK adopt a more participative and con-sultative style of leadership than their counterparts in Germany. Dutch managers are usually fairly relaxed about who is, or who should be, in charge; Germans, however, operate within a much more formal hierarchical structure and the French do not expect their decisions to be questioned when they are in a position of authority.

These national distinctions have been analysed by Hofstede (1980), using sociological dimensions such as power, risk, individualism and gender to create national models. The implications of Hofstede's research are that cultural differences do have a significant impact on how organisations operate, and also therefore on policies for managing people. For an excellent review of the implications of Hofstede's cultural categories for HR policies, see Schuler (2001).

Many organisations have equal opportunities or diversity policies that set out their commitment to provide equal opportunities for all categories of staff – according to the 2011 Workplace Employee Relations Study, more than three-quarters of workplaces now have a written policy on diversity and/or equal opportunities (van Woonroy and others 2013). However, for these policies to have an impact, line managers need to be proactive in ensuring that discrimination and unfairness is avoided and that differences are acknowledged, tolerated and indeed welcomed. Careful monitoring of diversity in the workforce can help you to identify areas where particular groups are underrepresented (by gender or ethnicity, for example) and this may alert you to discrimination either by the organisation (whether intentional or not) or by other workers. This could include bullying and harassment, practices which are sometimes pursued by managers, but much more frequently by workers or groups of workers against each other.

If differences are not well managed or understood, the result can be discrimination or conflict, which may develop into grievances or require taking some form of disciplinary action and possibly lead to legal consequences. We deal with this latter eventuality in Chapter 9.

Applying these ideas to your own experience

Think about people in your own area of responsibility. Which of them would you describe as 'different' from yourself in terms of gender, race or ability? What characteristics do you value in them?

Activities

1. Why do you choose to work in your present job? List your reasons in order of importance. Then ask some of your colleagues and subordinates what their reasons are – they may well be different from yours.
2. Does your organisation have an equal opportunities policy? If so, make a note of the responsibilities it gives you as a front-line manager in promoting equal opportunities.
3. Try to find out what monitoring your organisation carries out, if any, in relation to diversity issues. Can you learn anything from this monitoring about equal opportunities and diversity in the group of employees for whom you have management responsibility?

References

Acas, (2014) *Front Line Managers*. Advisory booklet. London, Acas.

CIPD, (2012) *Managing for Sustainable Employee Engagement: Developing a Behavioural Framework*. London, Chartered Institute of Personnel and Development.

Hackman J. R. and Oldham G. R., (1976) 'Motivation through the design of work: test of a theory', *Organizational Behaviour and Human Performance*, 16, 250–79.

Herzberg F., (1968) 'One more time: how do you motivate employees?', *Harvard Business Review*, 46(1), 53–62.

Herzberg F., Mausner B. and Snyderman B. B., (1959) *The Motivation to Work*. New York, John Wiley.

Hofstede G., (1980) *Culture's Consequences: International Differences in Work-Related Values*. London, Sage.

Maslow A. H., (1943) 'A theory of human motivation'. *Psychological Review*, 50(4), 370–96.

McLeod D. and Clarke M. (2009) *Engaging for Success: Enhancing Performance through Employee Engagement*. London, Department for Business, Innovation and Skills.

McGregor D., (1960) *The Human Side of Enterprise*. London, McGraw-Hill.

Open University, (2014) BB845 *Strategic Human Resource Management*, Unit 3, 'Employee engagement'. Milton Keynes, The Open University.

Purcell and Hutchinson, (2007) 'Front-line managers as agents in the HRM-performance causal chain: theory, analysis and evidence', *Human Resource Management Journal*, 17(1), 3–20.

Schuler R., (2001) 'International human resource management', in Storey J., (ed) *Human Resource Management: A Critical Text*, 2nd edition. London, Thomson Learning.

Storey J., Ulrich D., Welbourne T. M. and Wright P. M., (2009) 'Employee engagement', in Storey J., Wright P. M. and Ulrich D. (eds), *The Concise Companion to Strategic Human Resource Management*. Abingdon, Routledge.

Taylor, F. W., (1947) *Scientific Management*. New York, Harper and Row.

van Wanrooy B., Bewley H., Bryson A., Forth J., Freeth S., Stokes L. and Wood S., (2013) *Employment Relations in the Shadow of Recession: Findings from the Workplace Employee Relations Survey*. Basingstoke, Palgrave Macmillan.

5 Learning and development

Introduction

Learning and development can help to motivate employees and encourage them to make greater efforts to perform well, as you have already seen in Chapter 4. It is also important, in a knowledge-based and fast changing economy, that employees are willing and able constantly to upgrade their skills, and this means a commitment by both employers and employees to continuous learning, both individually and collectively, and to sharing the knowledge that is created through that learning.

Much of this learning will be work based, using reflection on practice and feedback (you began reading about this in Chapter 2 in relation to your own learning and development). Training courses and programmes still have their place and you will read in this chapter about ensuring that your staff get the most out of them, although there has been an important shift in most organisations away from training and towards an emphasis on continuous learning.

There has also been a shift towards providing learning and development opportunities tailored to the needs of the individual employer and often provided in the workplace. This is in recognition of the importance of making sure that skill development really meets the employer's needs and can be quickly translated into improved workplace performance. As a consequence, there is rather less use of generic training provision by external providers. There is also an increasing focus on using learning and development opportunities to surface, share and build on knowledge held by individual employees and to harness that knowledge to improve performance.

As a front-line manager you have a key role in supporting your staff in their learning and it is in your interests to do so since you are accountable for their performance and your success depends on their abilities. You will read in this chapter about approaches to identifying learning needs and about different approaches to supporting learning and development, including coaching and mentoring, e-learning and competency-based approaches. We will also look at the ways employers can be involved in skill development both in their organisations and more broadly, and at approaches of measuring, or evaluating, the success of learning and development interventions.

In this chapter we will be looking at:

- using learning and development to improve performance
- knowledge management
- encouraging continuous learning
- coaching and mentoring
- identifying learning and development needs and choosing methods to address these
- employers' role in skill development
- competency-based approaches to learning and development
- evaluating the results of learning, training and development.

Using learning and development to improve performance

The skills and motivations of the people who work in an organisation can make a dramatic difference to its ability to compete, and for this reason people are increasingly seen as the most important of its assets. You already know that good learning and development practices are associated with higher levels of workplace commitment and performance. More than this, however, a willingness to learn constantly and a commitment to lifelong learning can help organisations to change and develop quickly in response to a complex and fast changing external environment and to give them a competitive edge.

Senge (2006) pointed out the importance of continuous learning in organisations. This means not only that individuals must learn how to learn, but that they must work with others to create learning; and that the organisation's structures and processes must be designed to support this continuous learning. In this 'learning organisation' all members of the organisation are actively committed to learning, both individually and in teams, and would all be working towards a shared vision of the organisation's future. He described a learning organisation as 'a place where people are continuously discovering how they create their reality' (Senge 2006: 12).

You have already read about the importance of communication in Chapter 2, although it is worth reinforcing here its importance in supporting learning. Both listening and sharing ideas help learning to be created and knowledge to flow, and this means making time for discussion and for designing learning and development activities, which encourage the sharing of ideas and learning and provide opportunities for developing new understandings together. This often means facilitated learning events rather than events where information is given through lectures (although these do have their place). In 'open space' events, for example, all learning comes entirely from participants who learn simply from sharing each other's ideas and experiences.

Ben was looking forward to finding out more about coaching at the learning and development event organised by his company. The facilitator for the day was the HR director and managers from many parts of the company were present. He was very surprised when he arrived, however, to discover that no formal presentations were planned. Instead, attendees were invited to construct their own programme for the day and each was asked to make a presentation on an aspect of coaching which he or she knew about and would like to share with the other attendees. Ben himself spoke about his own experiences of being coached and the questions this had raised for him about how to coach his own staff. Those with more experience helped him to answer his questions and through others' presentations he learned about the way coaching was delivered in other parts of the company.

Knowledge management

If learning matters to organisations, so too does the knowledge that learning produces. Creation of knowledge and its application to finding new ways of working has long been recognised as an important source of competitive advantage. A distinction is often made between explicit and tacit knowledge (Nonaka 1994). Explicit knowledge can be articulated or written down, and can be relatively easily identified and recorded. Tacit knowledge, however, may be more ambiguous and harder to manage and to capture. It refers to the things that people in an organisation know but have never written down anywhere. One approach to capturing tacit knowledge is to find ways of sharing it so that it can be used more widely. This can be achieved through a range of approaches, closely linked to learning and development practices. Armstrong identifies these as including informal conferences, workshops, brainstorms and communities of practice (Armstrong 2012: 84). Communities of practice are groups of people who collaborate to share ideas and to develop new understandings related to their practice.

As a front-line manager you can contribute to this knowledge management in your own team by introducing practices, such as workshops, which encourage sharing of insights and understanding. You can also, importantly, create a culture in your team of openness and trust, which encourages this sharing and also making sure that you reward those who share their knowledge.

Human and social capital

Those who create and share knowledge in organisations, and who use it in their work, are of great value to the organisation, and they are sometimes referred to as its 'human capital'. The Chartered Institute of Personnel and Development defines human capital as 'the knowledge, skills, abilities and capacity to develop and innovate possessed by people in an organisation' (CIPD 2012: 1). There is increasing pressure on organisations to measure and report on the value of this human capital and the methods they are using to manage it, and many organisations do now report on human capital issues, although not yet using common measures and approaches (CIPD and ACCA 2009).

Social capital is a closely related concept. It has long been used in discussion of the value to communities of common ties of trust and common understandings and is now often applied to organisations to express the value to them of trusting relationships and networks between individuals and departments. The process of knowledge management depends on this social capital so that the two complement each other.

Applying these ideas to your own experience

Try to think of some areas of tacit knowledge in the work of your team. You may not be able to specify these exactly – tacit knowledge can be ambiguous. You may, however, be able to identify, for example, individuals who seem to be able to get things done in a way others, who may perhaps be less experienced, cannot. What could you do to try to surface and share this knowledge?

Encouraging continuous learning

An important aspect of continuous workplace learning is the ability to reflect on workplace practice and to think about how to do things differently next time. You can encourage those who work for you to do this by helping them to think, when things do not go well, about how they can be done differently and better next time. For this to work, you will need to avoid adopting a blaming or critical approach; if people are afraid to tell you when things have gone wrong you will have lost the opportunity to discuss reflectively with them how their performance could be improved. Your staff, like you, should be learning how to use reflection constantly to improve their workplace practice.

You can model good practice for those who work for you by the way you develop your own skills and work on improving your own performance in the workplace in the ways that you read about in Chapter 2. They should be using the same approaches as you in managing their own development and your example is the most powerful way of encouraging them to do so.

You will often have to give your staff feedback in order to improve performance. This will be an important part of the appraisal process (which you will read about in Chapter 7) but you should also make a practice of giving feedback regularly so that it feeds into a process of continuous improvement. To be useful, however, this feedback needs to be given both skilfully and sensitively. Most of us find it hard to give feedback (and it is equally hard sometimes to receive it); however, poorly delivered feedback is not likely to be productive.

Feedback should always identify specifically what has been done well (or less well); it should not be overlaid with blame or criticism, both of which are likely to provoke a defensive response. It is important to give positive and well as negative feedback, so the recipient learns what he or she has done well and could usefully do more. It can also be helpful to try to give positive feedback whenever you have to give feedback which may be less palatable.

Those who work for you may sometimes wish to give you feedback in turn, and there is a case for encouraging them to do so if you are serious about your development as a manager. This may be given skilfully or not, although if you listen carefully and ask for specific examples of whatever is the subject of the feedback, you will be modelling good practice in receiving feedback as well as getting the best learning you can from it. Once you are clear what is being said and have considered it, you may decide to act on it or to disregard it. Not all feedback is helpful, and you have to judge for yourself whether to act on it or not.

Applying these ideas to your own experience

Think about a time when you have received feedback about your work. If this feedback was helpful to you, what was it about the feedback or the way it was delivered that made it helpful? If it was not helpful, what was it about the feedback or the way it was delivered that made it unhelpful? Can you learn anything from this about how to deliver feedback well yourself?

Coaching and mentoring

Most organisations offer coaching and/or mentoring to their staff, according to the CIPD's *Learning and Development* survey (CIPD 2014). Both are essentially non-directive approaches to supporting learning, and both are important in supporting continuous learning. The differences between the two are not always absolutely clear. Typically, however, a mentor is usually a work colleague at the same or at a more senior level than the individual, to whom he or she can go to discuss work-related issues. A coach will be more directly focused on performance and skill development, often giving feedback to support this (CIPD 2013).

Mentoring

Mentors can pass on practical insight derived from experience and can pick up on new ideas and attitudes. They can help those they are mentoring to set themselves realistic expectations and steer them in the right direction as far as their career aspirations are concerned. It can, and should, be a mutually rewarding experience. Many people value being able to pass on what they know, particularly when this is appreciated and others benefit from their knowledge and experience.

An individual may have more than one informal mentor, different people to whom he or she can go for advice and help. This may be initiated by the individual who deliberately seeks out others from whom to learn, or it may be a formal mentoring arrangement whereby mentors are assigned to new staff as they are recruited. Both forms of mentoring have their benefits and disadvantages. A mentor chosen by the individual to be mentored will have the advantage over one who is imposed. On the other hand, not everyone is proactive in seeking a mentor and a formalised system at least ensures everyone has someone to whom they can go.

Although many organisations encourage informal and formal mentoring, fewer provide training for mentors, make time available in which to undertake this responsibility or give rewards. An untrained mentor, however, can have a disastrous effect and can actually reinforce bad practice rather than encouraging good performance. Mentoring does need to be managed professionally, with meetings arranged in advance, programmed into the diary and based on a clear agenda relating to the mentee's needs.

Rewards for mentoring are often intrinsic, in that mentors value the increased responsibility and gain satisfaction from helping others to achieve their potential. It is good practice to recognise the efforts mentors put into their work and to support them in turn in developing the skills they need to do this effectively.

Coaching

Coaching may be provided by internal or external coaches, although the former are more often used than the latter (CIPD 2014). To be effective, coaching needs to be planned and time should be allowed for the coach to develop staff. It involves consciously seeking out opportunities for developing people, training the person to do the job and giving him or her impartial feedback on performance. Like mentors, coaches must be well trained for their interventions to be useful; and like mentors, coaches can themselves learn a great deal from the experience of coaching.

Coaching and mentoring in the workplace are both expected to be focused on work or career issues, although inevitably there are times when performance is affected by personal issues, and these will find their way into coaching and mentoring sessions. When this happens, coaches and mentors may find they are dealing with an individual who is distressed and with issues that are outside their expertise. Problems that need professional help, such as alcohol or drug abuse, depression and serious personal and domestic problems, should always be referred to a specialist who is trained to give advice and help in these and other matters. It is potentially dangerous and damaging for an untrained person to attempt to intervene in these cases.

Those who provide coaching must have an opportunity to discuss their experiences of this confidentially either with peers or, ideally, with a more experienced coach. This is known as supervision and can help to improve coaching practice because it provides support and guidance about how to deal with issues raised in coaching. Supervision provides a valuable opportunity to explore dilemmas, including ethical dilemmas, where issues have been raised relating to welfare issues or management practice. For more on coaching supervision see CIPD (2006).

Neither mentor nor coach will normally be the individual's own line manager, although line managers may coach and mentor those whom they do not line manage. To work in either role you will need more guidance than can be provided in this chapter. However, you are also likely to have to use coaching and mentoring skills in a more general way, in managing those who work for you. This can be the case, for example, during the annual appraisal or performance review, particularly if you have to appraise someone who has been performing badly. This is a time when you have to get to the heart of what is causing inadequate performance – and the person being appraised may be reluctant to tell you or even be unaware of the cause himself or herself.

The first essential is to define the problem between yourself and the other person and ensure that you both understand what it is. This involves the skills of 'active listening', which you read about in Chapter 2. For example, an employee who is not performing up to standard tells you emphatically that it is the fault of the new machine, the new process or a new member of staff. Through careful and sensitive probing and attentive listening, you discover that the problem lies in lack of training or the employee's fear that someone else will take over their job. The next stage is to get the employee to recognise this, in a non-blaming way, so that neither of you identifies the employee as being at fault.

Once the problem has been redefined in a way that satisfies you both – and this is not always possible – you will need to be able to provide a solution which is mutually acceptable. This might involve offering learning opportunities or support of some other kind; it might, for example, involve ensuring that the person receives regular feedback on their performance, which reassures them that they are doing the job well or indicates ways in which they might improve their performance.

Throughout all of this, you need to gain the trust of the other person. That person needs to be sure that you have his or her interests at heart and that you are not likely to use the information you now have to the person's detriment. As a manager, you represent the organisation and sometimes the organisation itself has contributed to the problem, for example by not providing adequate support. In this case you and the organisation have some responsibility to help to find a solution.

Approaches to coaching and mentoring

Generally, in coaching and mentoring your purpose is to help employees to solve their own problems or make their own decisions. Here are some examples of the sorts of approaches you might use to help them to do this:

- the person-centred style: this depends on the manager 'reflecting' back to the other person the key issues and encouraging him or her to find the solution
- the supportive style relies on the manager being able to empathise with the employee, minimising feelings of isolation, guilt or weakness in the latter
- the interpretive style is more realistic than the supportive style since it recognises that the manager cannot always know what the other person is feeling. Instead of saying 'I know how you are feeling . . .', the manager using this kind of style would be more likely to say 'Is this how you are feeling – have I got it right?'
- the probing style is more appropriate for fact-finding, but there are often times when managers need to check facts and also to probe where they feel they are not hearing the whole story.

None of these approaches includes problem-solving or offering advice. This may be an approach you sometimes adopt as a manager, and you may find yourself slipping into this mode when coaching or mentoring. However, you are likely to find that successful solutions are most often found when those wrestling with the problem work out for themselves how to address it.

Applying these ideas to your own experience

Which of the above styles do you most often use? Can you think of times when it would not be appropriate?

Identifying learning and development needs and choosing methods to address these

As an employee of the organisation and as a manager you have a responsibility for the learning and development of the people you manage. This means planning and implementing an effective learning and development programme using resources from inside the organisation and, where necessary, external providers. It involves identifying, defining and assessing the competency levels of your staff, reviewing their development needs and career aspirations, and providing ways for them to learn and develop new skills. It also involves establishing, defining and reviewing objectives and performance measures, looking at the advantages and disadvantages of existing development provision and investigating new approaches.

Much of the work of assessing the competence of your staff and setting objectives for improvement through learning and development will be carried out through the staff appraisal system. This should also include carrying out a learning needs analysis in conjunction with the member of staff. Appraisal does not only involve assessment and objective-setting; it involves you in giving your staff constructive feedback on their performance and helping them to increase their potential. You will read more about this in Chapter 7, entitled Performance Management.

You will also need to look more broadly, however, at the skills you need in your team now and those you are likely to need in the future, and to consider the development needs both of individuals and of the group as a whole.

Learning and development methods

In practice, the forms of learning and development most commonly offered by organisations are on-the-job training and in-house development, and these are also regarded as the most effective (CIPD 2014). This has been strongly encouraged by the government as a way of boosting skills in the workplace and you will read more later in this chapter about employers' role in skill development.

You may choose to send employees on training courses, whether provided internally or by external providers. However, there are many other ways of providing opportunities for learning, often inexpensively. Coaching and mentoring, which we have already discussed, are obvious examples of this. Others include:

- *Job or work rotation.* This involves staff trying out a number of different jobs or different parts of the same job to get an understanding of other kinds of task and of how they all fit together. In either case, someone will have to be responsible for training the person in the new job or work.
- *Secondment.* This is a more formal type of job rotation in which a member of staff is seconded to another job on a short- or long-term basis, perhaps while someone is ill or when a member of staff has left.
- *Special assignments or projects.* This can mean finding ways of involving the person in different work, which may suit his or her particular skills or provide an opportunity to develop new skills.
- *'Sitting by Nellie'.* This form of learning exists in many organisations, notably those involved with production or manufacturing. The new employee is assigned to an experienced member of staff who should be given opportunities to develop skills in helping others to learn (although this does not always happen).

You may also consider using e-learning (sometimes known as online learning) and you will read more about this next.

E-learning and learning through social media

E-learning is widely used, particularly in larger organisations, to support learning and to create and share knowledge within the organisation. It has obvious appeal where large numbers of people, perhaps spread over a wide geographical area, have to be trained. It probably works best for short courses on technical or practical subjects such as health and safety and can have the advantages of being easily accessible and flexible so that it can be fitted into busy schedules. There are doubts about the effectiveness of e-learning (CIPD 2014), but since this term covers quite a wide range of approaches to learning this may simply be because the packages offered are sometimes poorly designed or used in situations for which they are not really suitable.

E-learning can incorporate interactive activities, which some students find helpful. They can include discussion forums which allow asynchronous discussions between students (that is, discussions not being held in real time); it is also possible to include sessions where individuals speak to each other face to face in real time – although clearly this requires considerable investment in equipment by the sponsoring organisation. Virtual reality training in simulated environments has also been available for many years and has been used to provide training in the emergency services, for example.

E-learning can also be used to complement face-to-face learning, by allowing students to complete a knowledge-based training course before they attend a face-to-face training event. This can make the face-to-face training event shorter and therefore less disruptive to participants' working lives and less expensive. This combination of e-learning and face-to-face learning is usually referred to as blended learning.

Even where your own organisation does not have the ability to provide e-learning opportunities itself (and this will normally be the case for small and medium-size organisations) you may be able to access relevant courses supplied by an external provider. The best known example of easily accessible courses, supplied free of charge, are the Massive Open Online Courses (MOOCs), which have recently emerged as part of the higher education landscape. The first UK-led MOOC learning platform in the UK, FutureLearn, was launched in December 2012 as a company owned by the UK's Open University but in partnership with many UK and international universities. The access MOOCs provide to free online learning potentially marks a major shift in access to learning, and the launch of FutureLearn was expected to revolutionise the higher education sector. It may also have potential to make an important difference to corporate learning. You can find more about FutureLearn and the open online courses offered through this platform on the FutureLearn website at www.futurelearn.com.

Social media can also provide opportunities for learning, and can support knowledge management within organisations. Wikis, for example, are now well established as a collaborative tool to share knowledge (the biggest and best known example of this is Wikipedia). They can also provide opportunities to share ideas and experiences and are often used to complement training courses. Twitter can be used to carry on the discussion between participants after they have left a conference or training event (or even before they have left). Blogs are also widely used to share ideas within organisations and many managers, including CEOs, now use them to make a constant flow of information and ideas available to those who work for them.

Applying these ideas to your own experience

Spend some time exploring MOOCs, using the internet. Can you see ways that any of the courses you have found could be used as part of your own personal development or to support the development of your staff?

Employers' role in skill development

Employers have a strong interest in supporting learning and development in their own organisations and, in the case of larger organisations, in contributing to skill development in the wider workforce from which they hope to recruit. Nonetheless there are, and have been for some time, concerns about the level of skills among the UK workforce, and successive governments have tried both to encourage employers to support learning and development in the workplace and also to ensure that qualifications for work-based training really reflect employer needs. Investors in People, for example, was introduced in 1991 as a government backed standard for people development and remains widely used in recognising good workplace practice. National Vocational Qualifications (NVQs) are also designed to support training and assessment in the competences actually used in the workplace and you will read more about these in the next section of this chapter.

A major review of skills in the UK, commissioned by the government and reporting in 2006, concluded that in spite of the efforts of previous governments the level of skills in the UK as a whole was too low to enable industries to compete effectively in the world marketplace and that a dramatic improvement in skill levels was needed. The report advocated major reforms in government policy on skill development (Leitch 2006) and subsequent policy changes brought employers right into the heart of skills development policy.

The UK Commission for Employment and Skills now provides guidance on employment and employment issues in the UK. It licenses 25 sector skills councils through which employers can contribute to the skill development of employees in their sector – some 85 per cent of employees in the workforce are covered by these councils. Their work includes updating the occupational standards (or competences) that form the basis of NVQs.

In some cases industries will join together to provide training which is tailored to the industry's needs. For example, the construction industry has its own industry training board, the Construction Industry Training Board (CITB), which works with the construction industry to encourage training. It is also a partner in the Sector Skills Council for the construction industry in England, Scotland and Wales, known as Construction Skills.

In 2008 McDonald's became one of the first employers to have its own in-house training accredited by the Qualification and Curriculum Authority (Harrison 2009) and employers can now, if they wish to, apply for the powers to award their own qualifications (once the preserve of universities and some professional bodies). This is in recognition of the fact that workplace learning is often the most effective way of developing the skills needed in the workplace (Leitch 2006). The government has also encouraged the development of in-house training for apprenticeship schemes. In hairdressing, for example, where once trainee hairdressers were sent on day release to local further education colleges, they are now often trained in-house by experienced practising hairdressers and have the opportunity to put their newly learned skills into practice straight away. This is illustrated in the case study below.

Sophie works as a hairdresser in a high street salon. She is a (very good) hairdresser herself and when she trained as a hairdresser she went to her local college to complete her initial training. Since then, however, things have changed considerably. Her salon now trains its own hairdressers using the national apprenticeship scheme. Sophie trains the apprentices in the salon to NVQ levels 2 and 3 and, having been trained as a NVQ assessor by an approved training provider, assesses their skills.

Sophie herself had trained by attending her local further education college on a part-time basis, starting by practising on model heads. While that training has certainly delivered good results in her case, she felt that there were considerable benefits in offering training in the workplace where trainees could immediately apply their learning to their practice.

The government continues to press for closer links between employers and training providers. In June 2014, Skills and Enterprise minister Matthew Hancock announced greater employer involvement in the design and funding of apprenticeships at the annual conference of the Association of Employment and Learning Providers. He promised that by September 2017 every new apprentice would be joining a scheme based on a standard designed by an employer and that funding for these apprenticeships would be put in the employers' hands (Churchard 2014).

Applying these ideas to your own experience

Does your employer offer apprenticeship schemes? If so, try to find out how they work and whether there is any potential for employing apprentices in your area of responsibility.

Competency-based approaches to learning and development

Competency frameworks set out the behaviours and skills that are required of individuals working in particular roles in an organisation. They are widely used, particularly in management and leadership development. Richard Boyatzis, in his 1992 book *The Competent Manager*, analysed these behaviours within five main clusters: goal and action management; leadership; human resource management; directing subordinates; and focus on others.

Since this seminal work became available to employers, many organisations have identified and described the competencies which they think most important in those who work for them. By publishing these competencies employers identify and describe the skills and behaviours they value in employees. Competencies can be linked to learning and development and, in many organisations, to a range of other aspects of managing people such as recruitment, induction, staff appraisal and promotion. They are also used to describe the requirements of particular roles and can be used in compiling person specifications.

You will find that the terms competences and competencies are often used interchangeably. However, a theoretical distinction has been made between them in the past, with 'competency' and 'competencies' used to describe the qualities that underpin performance and 'competence' and 'competences' used to describe those things you should be able to do in a particular role. Occupational standards are statements of competence in this second sense and form the basis of NVQs (or SVQs in Scotland). Occupational standards exist for managers, for example, the first occupational group for whom they were developed. These were originally drawn up by the Management Charter Initiative, set up in 1989, as part of an attempt to improve development opportunities for managers. Today these standards (now updated) are managed by the Management Standards Centre and you can find out more about them by looking at its website (www.management-standards.org).

National vocational qualifications are designed to be focused on employers' needs and have the great advantage that individuals can remain at work while they are training. One effect of their introduction has been the training of employees, often managers, as assessors for these qualifications. Organisations can now train their own staff, instead of sending them off to external providers, and can assess them in the workplace, as you saw in the hairdressing case study above.

Applying these ideas to your own experience

Does your organisation support the use of NVQs? If so, do you already use these as part of your own learning and development or encourage your staff to use them? If not, are there ways in which you could use them?

Evaluating the results of learning, training and development

The cost to any organisation of learning, development and training for its staff can be considerable. This may be an investment that pays dividends or it may simply be wasted expenditure. As a manager you will have to make judgements, as we have discussed, about how to allocate resources to these activities and you will need to be able to demonstrate that this has been done wisely and has produced returns for the organisation.

This is not an easy task. Employees may be able to demonstrate very quickly how their new learning will improve their own performance and contribute more widely to improving the performance of their group or section. However, this is not always the case and sometimes the results of learning activities may be hard to identify. This is particularly true of leadership and management development training, both of which typically seek to develop individual capability in ways which are not easily measured and may in any case take some time to produce an effect (although these courses may also include technical or practical skills which are easier to measure). The more immediate return may take the form of improved employee satisfaction, morale or engagement, which will hopefully translate into better performance later. You might look for these benefits by monitoring feedback from surveys of satisfaction, morale or engagement carried out by your organisation (where these exist) or by looking at other HR measures, such as sickness or absence. However, there will be many factors feeding into all these results and it is not likely to be easy to isolate the effects of a particular learning and development activity.

The most widely used approach to assessing the value of learning and development interventions, according to CIPD's learning and development survey (CIPD 2014), is simply to note changes in the way employees behave or act after a learning and development intervention. However, you can adopt a more systematic approach by looking for evidence of how much employees enjoyed the event, how much they learned from it and how relevant that learning is for their work. You could establish all of these through a discussion, perhaps at appraisal time. These are progressive levels of evaluation proposed by Armstrong (2012) and he added a fourth: the value of the learning to the organisation. This is difficult and is rarely done in a systematic way, but you might make a shrewd judgement as a manager about the value to the organisation of the way its money has been spent.

Applying these ideas to your own experience

Look back at the learning and development opportunities provided for those in your area or responsibility over the past year, including coaching, mentoring and e-learning. Which do you think have provided the best value for money and which criteria have you used to measure this?

Activities

1. Identify the learning and development needs for individuals within your area of responsibility.
2. Draw up a list of learning and development provisions which would meet the needs of staff you identified in (1) above, using internal and external training resources where appropriate.
3. Find out whether a competency-based approach is used in your organisation to define roles or for any other purpose. If so, how could you use these competencies to inform your choices about learning and development for yourself or those whom you line manage?

References

Armstrong M., (2012) *Armstrong's Handbook of Human Resource Management Practice*. London, Kogan Page.
Boyatzis R., (1992) *The Competent Manager*. New York, John Wiley and Sons.
Churchard C., (2014) 'Minister outlines apprenticeship reforms at AELP conference', *People Management*, 4 June. Available on-line at www.cipd.co.uk/pm/peoplemanagement/b/weblog/archive/2014/06/04/minister-outlines-apprenticeship-reforms-at-aelp-conference.aspx [accessed 20 July 2014].
CIPD, (2006) *Coaching Supervision: Maximizing the Potential of Coaching*. London, Chartered Institute of Personnel and Development.
CIPD, (2012) *Human Capital*. Factsheet. Available on-line at www.cipd.co.uk/hr-resources/factsheets/human-capital.aspx [accessed 20 July 2014].
CIPD, (2013) *Competence and Competency Frameworks*. Factsheet. Available on-line at www.cipd.co.uk/hr-resources/factsheets/competence-competency-frameworks.aspx [accessed 24 July 2014].
CIPD, (2014) *Learning and Development: Annual Survey Report 2014*. London, Chartered Institute of Personnel and Development.

CIPD and ACCA, (2009) *Human Capital Management: An Analysis of Disclosure in UK Reports*. Available on-line at www.cipd.co.uk/hr-resources/research/human-capital-management-disclosure-uk-reports-analysis.aspx [accessed 20 July 2014].

Harrison R., (2009) *Learning and Development*, 5th edition. London, Chartered Institute of Personnel and Development.

Leitch S., (2006) *Review of Skills: Prosperity for All in the Global Economy – World-Class Skills. Final Report*. Norwich, Her Majesty's Stationery Office.

Nonaka I., (1994) 'A dynamic theory of organizational knowledge creation', *Organization Science*, 5(1), 14–37.

Senge P. M., (2006) *The Fifth Discipline: The Art and Practice of the Learning Organization* (revised edition). London, Random House.

6   Leading teams and groups

Introduction

In Chapter 1 we noted the increasing recognition that leadership was a relevant dimension of the front-line manager's role and this is something we now expand on in differentiating between management and leadership. Leadership is often associated with change so that, as change becomes more prevalent and requires implementing and even initiating at the lower levels of management, we argue that leadership needs to be distributed throughout the organisation and not merely concentrated at the top. But we also argue that leadership is not simply about change in the sense of structural change but rather about incremental developments as well. Leadership styles are important, especially in suiting the style to the context. Also examined is the way in which your workforce might be organised, mainly into a group or a team, the behavioural tendencies of these and when a particular mode of organisation might be appropriate, with particular reference to the characteristics of teams. Then, having identified a suitable structure for your workforce, there are questions of selecting suitable people for the various roles, setting objectives and monitoring progress.

This chapter therefore covers the following topics:

- management and leadership
- leadership types
- leadership and management styles
- groups
- groups and teams
- teams
- forming an effective team
- team roles
- setting team objectives
- monitoring and evaluating progress
- leading a team.

Management and leadership

Frequent attempts have been made to distinguish clearly between management and leadership. At one simplistic level, it is said that management is about doing things right, whilst leadership is about doing the right things. On another dimension, it is often said that the difference between management and leadership is that leadership is manifested in a context of change, whereas management is about organising in a stable situation. We do not agree with this differentiation; we believe that leadership is not exclusive to change situations, just as we do not believe that leadership is exclusive to senior management, but can be relevant to front-line managers. Leadership can be about doing the same things better through motivating and inspiring people, just as it can be about doing new things or in a different way, whereas our view of management is about the effective operation of appropriate procedures and systems. This involves people, but not in the dynamic way that leadership can improve outcomes through motivated individuals and good relationships between people, usually in a team context.

A third differentiation comes from original definitions; classical management is usually defined in terms first articulated in 1916 by the French engineer Henri Fayol, as noted in Chapter 1, namely planning, organising, commanding, coordinating and controlling. These are primarily administrative functions. By contrast leadership, although subject to various different approaches to be outlined below, can be expressed through three more dynamic dimensions: providing for the unit (at whatever level) a vision and strategy to achieve it; aligning people in accordance with that vision; and motivating and inspiring them in pursuit of it, often in respect of change. Although such a description implies a formal structure and role, this not necessarily the case; leadership can be provided by someone not so designated in the authority structure, whether by someone with a particular aptitude in a particular context, or by leadership of an informal grouping outside the formal structure. The issue of informal groups in an organisation is an important part of organisational life and something we will discuss later in the chapter.

However, having tried to differentiate between leadership and management, we do not want to imply – which sometimes seems to be the case in modern writing – that management is dull, bureaucratic and lacking ambition, whilst leadership is exciting, challenging and charismatic. In fact, management and leadership are essentially two sides of the same coin. Both are necessary parts of organisational life, as appropriate in particular contexts.

Leadership types

There are many different types or approaches to leadership, contained in a huge literature on the topic, including:

- authoritarian – based on power, whether ownership or hereditary
- paternalistic – the father-figure as leader
- democratic – by the participation of the followers
- laissez-faire – by delegation or allowing events to take their course
- transactional – based on rewards and punishments for the followers
- transformational – charismatic leadership based on an inspirational vision.

There are numerous others, and the one which we will use, distributed leadership, is not part of this list. Of course, leadership has always been important since the dawn of history, and in all areas of human activity. Indeed, the eminent management scholar Peter Drucker (1954) has argued that we know no more about it now than was known by the ancient Greeks. However, recently its place in organisational life has been increasingly highlighted as the pace of global change has quickened.

There are almost as many theories about what makes a good leader as there are different kinds of people, and any attempt to identify the key attributes of leadership is likely to result in a wide range of answers (Mabey and Thomson 2000). Early research concentrated on trying to identify the personality characteristics of 'good' leaders – and failed. People who were considered to be successful leaders had different characteristics, different levels of intelligence and different skills. Later research looked at the way leaders behaved in different situations, but most experts in the field conclude that leadership cannot be explained simply by studying individuals. The leadership of a team needs to be related to the task which is being carried out, the needs of the team and the needs of individuals in that team, as well as the wider strategy being pursued.

To move to our own approach, we start from a rather different perspective than most approaches to leadership. This is distributive leadership, based on three different premises developed by O'Neill (2000a). The first of these is that leadership abilities can be developed, and that everyone has some untapped leadership potential. Second, O'Neill argues that leadership is diverse, namely that different leadership roles and different situations require different abilities. Third, leadership is distributed not concentrated at the top; modern organisations need leaders with diverse abilities at every level and in every quarter.

O'Neill argues that there are three main types of leader within the organisation. First, there is the visionary leader, exemplified by those at the top of the organisation, whose leadership role is to provide a vision, corporate values, structure and, if necessary, to transform the organisation, to ensure organisational survival and to please the shareholders. Such leaders need a conceptual, 'big picture', externally oriented mindset.

At the next level there is the integration leader, as with the head of a department, region or site, whose role is to link the unit into the corporate mission and vision, to develop the unit's system and process infrastructure, and to develop and champion a strong culture and leadership style within the unit, as well as reconciling conflicting interests and goals between units. Here the mindset is medium term, facilitating, boundary spanning and incorporating corporate values.

The third type is that of the fulfilment leader at the project, shift or team level, whose role is to please the customer or client, to deliver operating results on time, to make continuous improvements and increase the productive use of resources. In this context the mindset is short term, focused on quality and relatively immediate results, with customer service thinking and a human psychology. O'Neill therefore brings leadership down to the level of management, which is likely to incorporate your own role.

Applying these ideas to your own experience

Can you identify these types of leader within your own organisation?

However, it must be recognised that distributed leadership is not necessarily easy to install; it requires planning, integration and recognition by the whole organisation. Moreover, leadership may also need to be activated in different contexts, which can require different styles. Some may require a quick imposed decision, whilst others will be better served by a more consultative style of leadership. This raises the question of identifying different styles of leadership and their relevance to different situations.

Leadership and management styles

Again, this is a big topic, with styles being to some extent aligned with leadership types. Some styles have become well known by acronyms, such as MBO (Management by Objectives) and MBWA (Management by Walking About). You can review your own style in this section, bearing in mind also what you learned in Chapter 2 about yourself. O'Neill (2000b) suggests six different leadership or management styles.

Command: exercising strong central authority and retaining leadership and responsibility to oneself; setting the direction for others; expecting much of oneself. The main positives here are likely to be forcefulness in getting things done and meeting people's need for clear direction. The potential negatives are reducing other people's ability to make decisions and being seen as unfeeling about the people below you.

Control: results-oriented based on goal and target-setting, structure and hard discipline; being decisive and confronting issues head-on; uncompromising in standards. The positives here are clear targets aimed at high performance, problem-solving and getting results. The negatives are likely to be micromanagement, discouraging others and a tendency to blame when things go wrong.

Support: helping others unlock their potential; showing consideration and respect; listening, supporting and being there for others; trusting others and being trusted. The potential positives are bringing out the best in others and contributing to high morale and a learning culture. The negatives can be that tough decisions do not get made, that you can be too trusting and that people sometimes need to be told what to do.

Facilitate: enabling individuals, teams and processes to operate more effectively and make continuous improvements through communication, cooperation and problem-solving. The likely positives are building good relationships, providing stimulation and learning, and helping others to take responsibility. The negatives are that you sometimes need to be more demanding of staff and that your style of leadership may be seen as weak in a tough environment.

Hands-on: applying practical know-how and working together with the team; leading by example and responding to needs as they emerge. The potential positives are that your know-how enables you to cut through confusion, that by giving respect you will add to the self-confidence of your workers, and that you will be the keeper of high standards. The negatives are that being hands-on even to details, you miss out on the broader picture, that you may not delegate adequately and that you may spend time doing things that your staff should be doing.

Expert: providing technical and professional skills as a source of knowledge and advice; creating a non-confrontational climate for independent working. The positives here are that your specialist knowledge avoids pitfalls, that in your area of expertise you are a source of wisdom and that you can develop others. On the negative side, your knowledge may make you seem superior and condescending, whilst in providing solutions others may be discouraged from finding their own answers.

Although these descriptions define different approaches and everyone in a leadership or management role is likely to have a dominant style, individuals may use different styles according to the situation; indeed, no one style is appropriate for all situations or indeed for all people, since individuals respond differently to different styles of leadership. You need to understand the needs of the situation and the people involved, and your effectiveness is likely to be highest when your preferred leadership style matches the needs of the situation and the people. This leads to another of O'Neill's concepts, that of situational leadership and that successful leaders are able to adapt their style to the situation.

The appropriate styles for particular situations can be inferred from the descriptions above. Thus, the command style is appropriate when there is a crisis, or a conflict, or when people don't know what is expected of them, but inappropriate when staff need discretion to make quick decisions or take responsibility or develop themselves. Similarly, the control style is appropriate when standards or self-discipline are low or in unstructured situations lacking focus, but inappropriate when trying to build trust or commitment or improve communication or participation.

The support style is appropriate in contexts where the two styles above are not, namely in building trust and commitment, when morale and confidence are low, and when wanting individuals or groups to take greater responsibility, but inappropriate in crises or confused situations or when staff are uncooperative. Facilitation is appropriate when trying to build a high performance or service culture or where staff need to take the initiative, but inappropriate in tough negotiation situations where there have to be winners and losers or when urgent action is required and there is no time for consultation.

Hands-on is an appropriate style when the subordinates are not mature and competent or when the leader has both managerial and technical/professional responsibilities but not when unpopular decisions must be taken or staff are uncooperative. The expert style is appropriate when high technical standards are important or where a lot of leeway is given to staff because of their technical competence but not when there are divergent interests in the group or again when staff are uncooperative.

Goffee and Jones (2001) argue that there can be no leaders without followers and that followers essentially seek three dimensions of their leaders: significance to make them feel valued; community to make them feel a unity of purpose; and excitement to make them feel engaged. The role of followers has been under-estimated; ongoing success with weak followers will usually prove elusive. If it is true that an organisation is only as good as its leaders, it is also only as good as its followers. Moreover, of course, many managers, including front-line managers, are both leaders and followers, and this is part of the pressure of the role. Going back to O'Neill, the nature of the followers is an important part of situational leadership, and this leads us to examining the nature of groups and teams in which these 'followers' might be organised.

Applying these ideas to your own experience

Which of O'Neill's leadership styles do you recognise in your own style? Which do you not utilise?

Groups

A group is a number of people in a working situation who relate to a common goal and usually come within an area of managerial responsibility so that there is an element of structure but who do not necessarily interact together within their work activities. The traditional concept of a work group, often associated with production activities, has a front-line manager or supervisor who plays a strong role as the 'boss'. Each person in this work group has his or her own job and works under the close supervision of the 'boss'. The 'boss' is in charge and tells the employees the dos and don'ts in their jobs in something like the 'command' style of leadership noted above, whilst spontaneous initiatives such as helping each other or covering for one another do not often occur often. In fact, most problem solving, work assignments and other decisions affecting the group come from the manager.

However, in other types of work group, individuals use more of their own initiative, and this is probably the most common form of work group. Each person is still responsible for his or her own main area, but because the members have a reasonably high level of skill or professionalism, such as teachers in a school, the manager tends not to function like the controlling boss. Instead, staff members work on their own assignments with general direction and less supervision, whilst still requiring managerial guidance and support

Organisations create formal work groups for reasons concerned with the way in which work is structured. But organisations also breed informal groups which spring up despite, and sometimes in opposition to, the formal organisation. These may be formed by people who share a common problem at work or dissatisfaction with working conditions. For this reason they are often referred to as 'interest' groups since the members of the group share a common interest in work-related matters. They may be formed through some shared concern such as a desire for equal opportunities practices at work or the perceived need for a staff canteen or a non-smoking policy. Or they may be groups of people with shared interests and beliefs outside their work context – for example in voluntary work, amateur dramatics or a particular religion. These groups have no authority in the eyes of the organisation, although they can satisfy social needs and may create considerable pressure for change. There are trade-offs in being a member of a group. You may have to conform to behaviour which, as an individual, you are not used to or find difficult. However, your acceptance by such a group will depend on the extent to which you conform to its norms. If you do conform, you will be accepted as a group member and share fully in its activities.

A wide range of issues about the way the organisation works can be the subject of conversation amongst employees over lunch or during a coffee break, even though the people who take part in them do not see themselves as a member of an informal or interest group. However, informal groups can exist for reasons with little to do with work, often within 'office' politics. Group dynamics can also focus on the individual – how he or she is behaving, how he or she relates to other members of the group, what any person is contributing, whether individuals are seeking power or are opting out or whether some group members are being deliberately or unwittingly excluded. The essential ingredient for examining group dynamics is trust between its members so that anyone can speak openly about his or her feelings and reactions.

The task the group is undertaking usually assumes prime importance, particularly when groups are competing with each other on the same task. It happens in organisations too, when different project teams are competing for additional resources or individuals are seeking rewards. In particular, ambitious and confident people can run away with the task without realising that what they are doing is not necessarily the only or best way of tackling it. Since they do not listen to others in the group, they are not using the potential resources that a group of people brings to any problem.

There are a large number of factors which interact to determine how effective – or ineffective – a group may be. These include:

- the size of the group
- group membership characteristics
- the stages of its development
- the task the group has to undertake
- the kind of organisation in which the group is working
- the group leader
- group processes and procedures
- group communication.

Groups and teams

Another type of work group relies on other members to get the work done, coordinating with one another to produce an overall product or set of outcomes. With this interdependence a team is formed. Whereas groups have individual goals, teams have collective goals and, moreover, the whole is greater than the sum of its parts. The team can be seen as a link between the goals of the individual and those of the organisation. However, it takes more time and effort to get a group of individuals to work as a team than to have a group of individuals pursue their independent assignments. Yet when teams capitalise on interdependence, they can outperform other types of work groups and they have become very popular as a mode of working where this is appropriate.

Not every group is a team, since many individuals in groups have roles which are not dependent on others, but teamwork has become an important part of organising work wherever it is appropriate because it implies the virtues of cooperation, interdependence and cohesion. A team may cut across existing functional divides or its members may be geographically remote from each other. It may involve diverse skills and comprise people from diverse backgrounds. Indeed, a person may be a member of more than one team. But a team requires a sense of belonging which separates the team from others. Harnessing this sense of interdependence and belonging requires leadership, as well as management at whatever level of the organisation the manager is operating.

Team leadership is usually participatory, in contrast to the primarily manager-driven nature of regular work groups. On a team, the manager or team leader frequently involves team members in helping shape the goals and plans for getting the group's work done – may as well get them involved, they've got to do the work! However, in other kinds of work groups, managers more commonly work with staff individually to set goals and determine assignments. Of course, in many cases, managers simply assign work with little discussion or collaboration with the staff members. And staff are then left to work out what's expected and how best to get it done.

Teams

Many of us are so used to working as part of a team that we fail to recognise what benefits accrue from effective teamwork and the dynamism which well managed teams bring to organisations. People working in teams draw upon each other's strengths to complement individual weaknesses. Indeed, team spirit in itself can act as a strong motivating force for personal improvement and for loyalty to the employing organisation. Working in teams affords the opportunity to develop new areas of competence and different skills, and failure, as well as success, can be shared. In organisational terms, working in teams can produce substantial improvements in areas such as morale, job satisfaction, productivity and quality. Teamworking has often been thought of as being connected with manufacturing, but it is capable of much wider application in almost any area of an organisation.

There are many different types of team. Thus, there might be an executive team at the top of an organisation, a project team to carry through a particular activity, an advisory team brought together to provide complementary sources of advice and, of course, the work team, with which you are most likely to be involved. However, there are also some more recently evolving types of work team, which may well become more significant. One of these has been the idea of self-managed and self-directed teams, where team members take on many of the functions of managers and supervisors. A self-managed team is where people work together in their own ways toward a common goal which is defined outside the team. Here the team does its own training, work scheduling, rewards etc. A self-directed team goes even further and is a group of people working together in their own ways toward a common goal which the team defines, and in addition to work scheduling the team also handles compensation, discipline and acts as a profit centre by defining its own future. Clearly, such teams can only operate in an organisational culture that encourages empowerment. At present they are largely experimental and conceptual, although they are likely to develop further in the future.

A second development, already quite well established, is the virtual team, sometimes also called networked teams, a group of individuals who work across time, space and organisational boundaries with links strengthened by webs of communication technology and who may never meet face to face. Virtual teams allow companies to utilise the best talent without geographical restrictions, but there are obvious potential problems of coordination, culture, cohesion, technical expertise, task processes and emotional linkages. Again, empowerment and, of course, effective leadership are necessary.

Perhaps the greatest interest has focused on a third development – high performance teams (HPTs) – in which major change is created through changing organisational culture by merging the business goals of the organisation with the social needs of the individuals. Katzenbach and Smith (1993) identified four characteristics – common commitment, performance goals, complementary skills and mutual accountability – which created the basis for a successful HPT. Owing to its initial success, many organisations attempted to copy HPTs. However, without properly understanding the underlying dynamics that created them, and without adequate time and resources to develop them, most of these attempts failed. Nevertheless, work continues to identify the key processes and team dynamics necessary to create performance improvements.

Teamwork is seen as a way of improving productivity and quality and employee motivation and commitment. It can achieve these objectives by utilising the different strengths and skills of team members, by permitting the team to take responsibility for control and tasks, and reducing the need for supervision. Involvement is a key to effective team working, and teams with some autonomy are likely to implement their solutions to problems more successfully. Traditional production techniques requiring simple tasks are often being replaced by more complex interactions. On the other hand it can create problems of demarcation about roles.

Although you may have inherited existing teams in your work, or become a member of an existing team yourself, you are likely to become involved in setting up work teams at some time or another. To do this, you will need to identify the skill or competence requirements needed and available in team members in relation to the demands of the task. Having selected the members of your team, you, as manager, need to establish and agree objectives for team development and working. This may involve using project planning and resource allocation techniques, the details of which are beyond the scope of this book. You will also need to define and allocate workload responsibilities and authority within the team and ensure that you give members of your team constructive feedback on their performance.

In order to maximise team performance, you will need to motivate your staff to reach the team's objectives and provide for learning and skill development where necessary. Managing a team involves establishing good relationships with all its members through genuine consultation and the establishment of clear lines of communication. This involves not only communicating 'outwards' to others – giving instructions, setting deadlines and so on – but being receptive to 'inward' communication from team members and others. Only by doing this can you assess information which is important and appropriate for your team to receive. You are also likely to lead team meetings and some advice on that was provided in Chapter 2.

Forming an effective team

An effective team will have certain key characteristics:

- a sense of common purpose
- clear goals
- good communications within the team
- open relationships between members
- A willingness to debate and discuss issues
- mutual trust and support for each other
- complementarity of personalities
- high motivation
- clear procedures and decision-making processes
- leadership appropriate to the needs of the team
- a regular review of operations, seeking to learn from experience
- cooperative relations with other groups.

Applying these ideas to your own experience

Think of a team of which you are either the leader or an active member. Using the above list as a check, identify which characteristics of your team are present and how effective – or ineffective – it is.

This, then, is what you should be aiming for when setting up and developing a team. It is of course a tall order, and even then there could be reasons for failure which might not be due to the team itself; for instance, although the goals may be clear, they may be in some way inappropriate. Your job will be easier if you are able to select team members yourself based on the demands of the task and the skills and competences required to complete it in a way which makes use of the various strengths of the team members.

In Chapter 3 on recruitment you were introduced to the idea of job descriptions and person specifications. The same techniques can be used to identify the activities the team has to carry out and the types of people that would be necessary to effect them. However, as you will see in the next section, you also have to take into account the balance of people in your team and the kinds of characteristics possessed by individuals. Of course, this assumes an ideal situation in which you are free to choose who will be in your team and those you select are both able and willing to be in it. Organisational reality means that you often have to include certain people because of their work role or place in the hierarchy or that the people you want are already committed to other projects or work.

As leader of a new team, you have to analyse the task it is expected to perform and the skills you will need; to do this you will need a form of 'job description', which sets out the requirements of the task. For example, suppose you were asked to set up a team of people to assess different types of computer software and introduce the preferred option into your department or organisation. You might draw up a description of the task in the following way:

Objective: To implement the most appropriate software program into ... within a period of x months at no more than y cost (of course, your time scale and budget may not be determined at this stage).

Method:

- identify current and forecast future software needs of department/ organisation
- identify appropriate commercial software packages
- test software packages
- consider design of package if no appropriate commercial package available
- select or design appropriate software
- load software on to hardware
- train staff in use of software
- evaluate implementation.

This would only be a very rough first shot at defining the team's task. Once the team is set up, you may have to redefine it in the light of more knowledge about what has to be done.

Looking at this rough description, it is obvious that you are going to need people with computing skills and, possibly, with the competence to design custom-made software. But you are also going to need people who can communicate what the team is doing to others outside the team. You will need to identify the current and future needs of people who will be using the new package. These people may be concerned about their ability to operate it, particularly if it is very complex and/or specialised; they will need reassurance. You will also need people who are good at helping others to learn, not simply people who are good operators. You will also need team members who are willing to undertake the rather unexciting work of testing the software packages ... and so on.

Your team member 'person specification' grows by the minute and large teams are less effective than small ones. Of course, you can always elect to work in sub-groups but you need to ensure that people who are going to be working together in small groups not only have the required competence but can work together. If possible, you will want to reduce the risk of interpersonal conflict within the group.

Team roles

One way of deciding upon who should join your team is to look at the team role that a person can play quite apart from his or her particular expertise. Belbin (2004), whose work on management teams is well known, differentiates between functional roles such as computer analyst, sales manager, accountant and so on, and team roles which relate to an individual's contribution to the effectiveness of the team. By identifying the particular roles team members can play and by recognising individual strengths and weaknesses in relation to these roles, you can build a well balanced and effective team. One of Belbin's early findings was that putting the brightest people together was not a recipe for success; indeed, the reverse. Far more important was the complementarity of different personalities who could each contribute to the outcome. This meant not too much similarity in personality, not too much in the way of polar opposites, but an input of certain characteristics such as creativity and an ability to get the job done. Individuals are usually strong in some aspects and weak in others. The same person can, therefore, perform more than one role in a team.

The important point is that teams which are well balanced in terms of the roles team members play will be more effective than teams which are imbalanced and where one or more essential team roles are missing. On a somewhat parallel point the management consultants Hay found that those in outstanding teams were not brighter, more driven or more committed than members of less successful teams but rather these people contributed emotional intelligence – the ability to understand the emotional make-up of others and empathise. At the same time, in focusing on the strengths that people bring to a team, their weaknesses should not be forgotten, even if to some extent these can be compensated for by the strengths of others.

The concept of team roles helps to identify imbalances in groupings of employees and, where there are gaps which need to be filled, this knowledge can contribute towards your determination of human resource requirements and inform future recruitment, selection and development of staff. Shortfalls in communication can be highlighted both within the team itself and between one team and another, increasing awareness of areas outside its own sphere of responsibility and generating general understanding of the wider organisational context.

Applying these ideas to your own experience

Consider in your team or a team that you know well what the complementary strengths are that each member brings to the team, and what the team is lacking.

Unfortunately, in real life teams are not always well balanced, and some teams are more effective than others. You should be able to recognise the shortcomings in any team of which you are a leader or a member. When you are setting up a team, it is useful to spend some time asking everyone to identify their own strengths and weaknesses and to discuss these with other team members. As a result, as a team you will be aware of any general weakness, such as not having anyone whose strength lies in communicating with others or being short of creative ideas. If you work in a team most of the time, this should also give you some guidance about the kinds of people you need to recruit.

Setting team objectives

Just because you are clear about what the team has to achieve – its allotted task – does not necessarily mean that all the members of the team either understand this or necessarily agree with it. Very early in forming a team you need to allocate time to set objectives which everyone is clear about and which can be realistically achieved. The whole team has to be involved in this if you are to get agreement and commitment from everyone. The following box is an example of the issues involved.

> Alison was asked to head up a team to look at staff development in a small company. She was given a budget for training and three members of staff from different parts of the company to work with her. At their first meeting, she explained their objectives as being to use the budget to provide the maximum amount of essential training within the next 12 months.
>
> At the second meeting she encountered considerable resistance to her ideas, although she thought everyone had agreed with what she had said earlier. Mira, from Sales, claimed that most of the budget should be used for training her staff since, unless sales improved, company financial objectives would not be met. John argued strongly for management training to improve performance; Trish insisted that customer service staff badly needed training since they were often the first contact for potential customers. The meeting broke up without anything being agreed and with each member of the team feeling personally aggrieved.
>
> At the next meeting Alison suggested they went back to basics and agree what their objective was in general terms before looking at ways in which they could achieve it.

Organisational objectives are often deliberately vague. At the operational, team level objectives need to be clarified and the team's resources and constraints determined. Once the team has agreed on its overall objectives, the business of putting together an action plan to achieve those objectives is the next step.

In the example above, the team's main constraint was financial, so they went on to look at learning and development options which would not require money, such as in-service training. (You read about examples of these in Chapter 5.) They identified people in the organisation who could contribute to training others and act as mentors to junior staff. They drew up a training plan for each department within the overall budget and also made recommendations for the budget to be increased in the following year. They also set up ways in which the training and its effectiveness could be monitored and measured and built in a number of review points so that changes to the original action plan could be made in the light of experience.

Monitoring and evaluating progress

Most teams are drawn together to work over a period of time – anything from a few months to years. One reason for setting objectives is that, over time, the team can check on its progress towards those objectives and, if necessary, make adjustments to the original plan. Things change. Even in a matter of months a team may find that the original plan was too ambitious or that unexpected hitches keep occurring which slow down progress. Key people may leave the organisation and not be replaced immediately, or at all; a sudden crisis may erupt, throwing the team off course; there may be a senior management reshuffle and priorities may change. Teams can build in 'slack' for unpredictable events and hold-ups but they do not know when or where these will occur. So it is very important for the team to take time at regular, scheduled intervals to check on how it is progressing.

However, setting aside time for review is not particularly productive unless you have some way of measuring progress, and you need to establish some kind of monitoring process early on. Ideally, all objectives should be measurable and you and your team should aim to set out not only what you intend to achieve, but how you can tell whether you have achieved it.

Let us take some objectives and see how they might be measured. For example, a team might have objectives so that it can:

- reduce production faults by 50 per cent
- decrease customer complaints to a minimum
- improve staff morale.

The first objective, reducing faults, sounds as if it could be measured, but how much is 50 per cent? You would need at least a base monthly figure of reported faults as a yardstick so that you could check on whether faults were being reduced over the period and that the rate of reduction was being maintained and improved in line with your objective.

And how do you measure customer complaints? Are they all reported or are some anecdotal? You would need to set up a system to record the complaints and probably qualify these as 'serious', 'less serious' and so on. You would then need to monitor the rate of complaints over time to evaluate whether they were decreasing.

The final objective of improving staff morale is much more difficult to measure in concrete terms but it is nevertheless important and goes back to some of the soft skills identified in Chapter 2, reading the 'vibes' through empathy and organisational intuition. As you saw in Chapter 4, individuals are motivated by different things and there is no 'staff morale improver' which you can buy off the shelf.

The main tasks for your team in relation to objectives are therefore to ensure that the team can:

- clarify and agree overall objectives
- consider options for achieving objectives
- set out, step by step, how the team plans to meet their objectives
- agree how to measure progress
- set a time scale and establish review points
- monitor and evaluate progress against measures
- adjust plans if necessary.

Team meetings are forums for planning work, solving work problems, making decisions about work and reviewing progress. In short, meetings are vital to a team's existence. We have discussed how you as a manager should run meetings in Chapter 2.

Leading a team

Team leadership is not always vested in the person who has been given that position by the organisation. It may change hands depending on the situation. For example, there will be times when the team needs to be led by a specialist if it encounters technical or other specialised difficulties; at other times it may be led by someone who has had previous experience of a particular type of problem or project. The best teams profit from the strengths of individual members and recognise when 'leadership' should pass to the most appropriate person. However, someone usually has the responsibility and title of 'team leader', at least in the eyes of the organisation, and is accountable for the team's performance.

As was pointed out earlier, the kind of task the team has been set and its timescale will often determine who should lead the team. However, the requirements of the task alone are not enough; the team as a group has needs which must be met and individuals within the team have their own needs. People make statements such as 'What we need is leadership' or 'The team needs direction' when they are articulating what the team as a whole feels is lacking.

Sometimes teams feel they need support, or feedback, or better communication and they look to the leader for all these things. Within the team, individuals also have their own needs – remember Maslow's hierarchy of needs in Chapter 4. The leader needs to be aware of individual needs and fulfil these as well, and this in most cases will mean having a facilitative style of leadership. One of the best ways of motivating people is enabling them to feel that they are participating, rather than being under a command and control style of leadership (see O'Neill's different styles). In fact, according to the Acas pamphlet entitled *Teamwork: Success Through People* (2005), the optimum leadership style should move from controller to initiator, facilitator and mentor by:

- providing a vision and communicating it
- encouraging the free flow of ideas and initiative
- training and developing teams to take increased responsibility
- ensuring the teams meet objectives.

One useful way of looking at the needs of the team is to use a simple diagram of interlocking circles involving task, group or team, and individual needs.

The three-circle model leads to questions about the three components:

- What is the purpose of the task?
- How is the task broken down into objectives?
- How are the purpose and objectives communicated to the group or team?
- What are the parts of the group or team?
- How do the parts contribute to the purpose?
- How do the parts relate together as a group or team?
- Do the individual parts have adequate discretion?
- Are the needs of individual members being met?

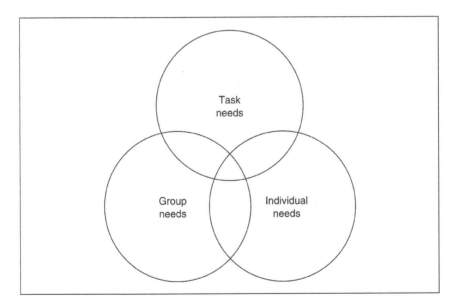

Figure 6.1 The three-circle model

Applying these ideas to your own experience

Think of a team of which you are a member. Does the leader consider the needs of the task, the team and the individual? In which areas is he or she (a) strongest, (b) weakest? Does the three-circle model help you to identify where this person may be lacking in leadership skills?

Activities

1. Looking at your own role. How much of your work would you designate as involving leadership rather than management?
2. For a team of which you are the leader or an active member, set out its:

   (a) general objective
   (b) operational plan
   (c) measures of progress
   (d) systems of monitoring and evaluation of progress.

References

Acas, (2005) *Teamwork: Success Through People.* Advisory booklet. London, Acas.
Belbin R. M., (2004) *Management Teams: Why They Succeed or Fail,* 2nd edition. Oxford, Elsevier.
Drucker P., (1954) *The Practice of Management.* New York, Harper and Row.
Fayol H., (1949 [1916]) *General and Industrial Management* (trans. Storrs). London, Pitman.
Goffee R. and Jones G., (2001) 'Followership: it's personal, too', *Harvard Business Review,* December, 148.
Katzenbach J. R. and Smith D. R., (1993) *The Wisdom of Teams: Creating the High-Performance Organization.* Boston, Harvard Business School.
Mabey C. and Thomson A., (2000) *Achieving Management Excellence: A Survey of UK Management Development at the Millennium.* London, Institute of Management.
O'Neill B., (2000a) *Test Your Leadership Skills.* London, Hodder and Stoughton.
O'Neill B., (2000b) *Leading the Way: Your Leadership Style and How to Develop It.* Northampton, The Innovative Management Partnership.

7 Performance management

Introduction

Managing the performance of staff is one of the most important functions of a front-line manager. The front-line manager is the person that most staff identify as the immediate face of the organisation and therefore its policies and attitudes. From the wider perspective, the company depends on its front-line managers to achieve the desired performance from the workforce through engagement, involvement and the use of soft skills. Managing performance is an ongoing activity, which provides direction, monitors and measures performance and takes any necessary action, and this is true at all levels in the organisation; indeed, in a real sense, it is what the organisation is all about.

The term 'performance management' incorporates managing performance but is also used to describe a cycle of events to achieve objectives, and it is this with which this chapter will be mainly concerned. The more closely aligned the cycle of events is with the day-to-day activities, the more successful both performance management and managing performance are likely to be. Both concepts are carried out at all levels of the organisation, but because front-line managers deal with the largest body of the workforce, their success depends largely on the ability of this group. Perhaps inevitably, dissatisfaction with the performance appraisal system centres mainly on the performance of front-line managers and a policy-practice gap (Purcell and Hutchinson 2007: 13). Just how many organisations use the full performance management framework is uncertain, but according to the 2011 *Workplace Employee Relations Study* (van Woonroy: 2013) 69 per cent of employees had an appraisal, which may be considered the key starting point of the system.

This chapter contains the following topics:

- the principles of performance management
- stage 1 – the plan
- stage 2 – development
- stage 3 – performance and its measurement
- stage 4 – review
- appraisal systems
- managing rewards
- problems and successes of performance management.

The principles of performance management

The main intentions of performance management are:

- It translates organisational goals into individual, team and unit goals.
- It helps to clarify the organisational goals.
- It provides a process for measuring outputs compared with objectives but also examines the inputs needed to achieve the objectives.
- It relies on consensus and cooperation rather than control or coercion.
- It encourages self-management of individual performance.
- It is about establishing a culture in which individuals and groups take responsibility for their own contributions.
- It is about improving relationships between managers, groups and individuals.
- It is about planning and measurement.
- It is a continuous and evolutionary process, and achieves improvement over time.
- It is strongly associated with development and especially identifying what development is needed.

At one level performance management is strategic in that it is concerned with integrating the different dimensions of an organisation's operations into its wider objectives, but it is also concerned with the role of the individual manager and, indeed, expects responsibility to be shared by all members of the organisation. The integration is primarily vertical, aligning organisational, team and individual objectives, but can also be functional, bringing together functional strategies in different parts of the organisation and within functions, such as integrating different aspects of managing people.

The aim of performance management is continuously to improve the performance of individuals and that of the organisation. It involves making sure that the performance of employees contributes to the goals of their teams and the business as a whole. The system is operated on an annual cycle which evaluates the past, sets future objectives, plans for the development needed to achieve those objectives, and potentially links to a framework of rewards, whilst there is also an ongoing record of progress and constant feedback on performance. This annual cycle is central to the whole concept of performance management, which has four distinct stages, although the review and the plan stages are usually carried out at the same time through the appraisal system, whilst the develop and perform stages are carried out continuously throughout the year.

To amplify these points, good performance management helps everyone in the organisation to know:

- what the business is trying to achieve
- their role in helping the business achieve its goals
- the skill and competencies they need to fulfil their role
- the standards of performance required

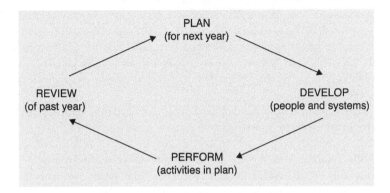

Figure 7.1 Conceptual performance management cycle

- how they can develop their performance and contribute to the development of the organisation
- how they are doing
- when there are performance problems and what to do about them.

The role of front-line managers in the performance management cycle is as follows:

- agree objectives, competencies and development needs with individuals
- review individuals' performance
- give feedback and discuss amendments with individuals as circumstances change
- agree a personal development plan
- assist individuals with coaching
- manage under-performance
- hold an annual appraisal with individuals
- write an appraisal report in collaboration with the individual employees.

Stage 1 – the plan

The first stage of a conventional performance management cycle is the plan. Broadly speaking, this identifies future performance requirements in terms of targets, actions and behaviours. The plan should challenge the individual but also be achievable. Ideally, it should allow that person to combine existing expertise with their potential for development. Plans must also address the alignment of priorities, including those of the individual, their team and the organisation as a whole. For the plan to work it also requires focus, both on what is to be achieved and how that is to be done. Finally, the plan requires commitment from all involved.

For any system to work effectively, it must be purposefully planned, with commitment at all levels, including at the senior levels. Objectives must be agreed with all concerned, incorporating the necessary competencies to implement the objectives. It is particularly important that the individual employee should be given the opportunity to contribute to his or her own plan, rather than merely being told what is expected. Good communication of how the system is expected to work is the next step, and training in the skills needed to make it work a further necessity. Since the front-line managers are the ones who will carry through the cycle with the workforce, it is particularly important that they should have adequate training to make the system work.

The starting point is an individual performance plan (IPP), with objectives that should be 'smart', namely:

- specific – a target which is clear, unambiguous and not too general
- measurable – concrete criteria for reaching the target, desirably but not necessarily quantitative
- achievable – realistic even if stretching
- relevant – criteria that really matter in the context of the job
- timebound – a target date to have a sense of urgency, rather than dragging on into the future.

Thus, it would be 'smart' to say 'answer all customer enquiries within two days' but not 'smart' to say 'answer all customer enquiries as quickly as possible'.

The IPP will also include key skills and a personal development plan (to be discussed below). Involving the employee in the creation of the plan, including the objectives, is likely to make them more relevant, acceptable and understood. Indeed, understanding the objectives is central to their success. Where groups are carrying out the same objectives it will be better to have a common discussion to prevent individual differences in understanding. The way in which the objectives are to be achieved also needs to be discussed. Thus, in a retail situation, how an employee relates to customers may be central to customer satisfaction, but objectives are likely to be measured in terms of sales, which may at least in the short term encourage an aggressive method of selling, which may get results but not provide optimum customer satisfaction.

The main ways in which the plan is structured is likely to be in terms of objectives and targets defining the outcomes expected, and in competencies or statements of what the individual ought to be able to do. But there are other considerations that the plan might include, such as relating to the written job description, or accountabilities for which the individual in question is responsible, or wider aspects of the job within the organisation.

Stage 2 – development

The issue of development has already been discussed at some length in Chapter 5, so here its focus is on its role within the performance management cycle. The second stage of a basic performance management cycle is the development of the individual's expertise and potential. The development phase should focus on both improving current expertise, and on allowing new skills or knowledge to be gained, particularly where there is evidence of potential. At this stage it is necessary that the manager identifies opportunities, then provides coaching and other support as needed (or available).

Employees should have a personal development plan (PDP), which can be discussed and modified at the appraisal interview. It is based on current strengths and weaknesses, incorporates personal aspirations in the short, medium and long term, and identifies what is needed to move forward. For each area of development, usually specified in competencies, there needs to be a means of achieving the development, a timescale for doing so and a record of achievement to date. There should also be an element of continuing professional development and career planning to help employees realise their potential and to ensure that skills are up to date. The PDP is something which individuals can carry with them throughout their careers, and from one employer to another. Surveys have shown that employees value development highly, since they see it as important for their future career.

As a manager, you are accountable for the performance of your staff and your success depends on their ability. Better trained staff should increase efficiency and even productivity by reducing fatigue and wastage. The starting point is to identify training and development needs for individual members of staff. Each individual for whom you are responsible is likely to fall into one of three categories in relation to his or her competence to perform the job. These are:

1   Competent to perform current job.
2   Not yet competent to perform current job.
3   Better than competent at performing current job.

For each category you can provide development as shown in figure 7.2.

The Acas Advisory Booklet *How to Manage Performance* (2014) suggests some competencies which are commonly used by organisations for their staff; there is, of course, a very wide range of actual and potential competencies. These overlap with but are not the same as the competences identified for front-line managers in Chapter 1:

- knowing the business
- communicating effectively
- embracing change
- focusing on goals
- developing self and others
- leadership
- teamwork
- creativity
- planning and organising
- equality.

These competencies can then be divided into levels of achievement. As well as these positive competencies it is also possible to have negative behaviours to be corrected, such as 'impatient with customers' or 'poor spelling and grammar'.

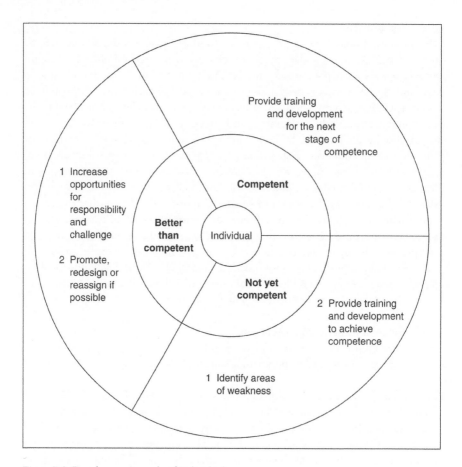

Figure 7.2 Development needs of individuals

Stage 3 – performance and its measurement

There are several factors to consider when managing the way people perform. First, plans and potential can count for little unless they are used to deliver something tangible. In a work-based performance management cycle, this must relate to the needs of individuals, their teams and their organisations. Second, there is deep satisfaction to be found in doing something well, and it is much easier to excel when using your strengths. Good managers ensure they help their colleagues do just that. Allow and encourage your people to do what they do best, preferably on a regular basis. Underpinning both of these points, ensure your people have the resources they need to be able to perform. Clearly, there may be limitations beyond the manager's control here. Nonetheless, it is unfair to expect improved performance without the right tools to enable it.

A key issue is how can performance be measured, bearing in mind the old dictum 'If you can't measure it, you can't manage it'? The following are some of the main ways in common use:

- Output rating, as with achievement of sales or quality targets or levels of budgeted expenditure.
- Achievement against objectives, in which the manager assesses with the employee the extent to which agreed objectives have been achieved.
- Behaviourally based rating scales, which focus on the behaviours rather than the outputs which are desirable for good performance.
- Competences or competencies, as discussed above.
- Critical incidents, in which the focus is key incidents of performance, both positive and negative.
- Narrative reporting, in which the manager describes the employee's performance in his or her own words.

However, there are also some issues which a good performance management system can contribute to, but which it cannot necessarily measure. Morale and motivation are intangible dimensions of organisational life, whilst many important outputs can only be measured on a group rather than individual basis. Moreover, while evaluation of performance can provide a rating, it is not easy to translate this into pay or other rewards.

A different way of looking at measurement is what is measured, as with the following:

- Financial, as through cost, income, value added, rates of return, shareholder value.
- Output, such as sales achieved, new accounts opened, units produced.
- Reaction, such as views of other managers or workers, or clients or customers.
- Impact, as with changes in behaviour, achievements of given standards, completion of activities, innovative developments.
- Time, such as speed of response or delivery, turnaround times, levels of backlog.

The issues to be measured ought not to have a single focus, otherwise the employee will tend to concentrate on that to the detriment of other aspects of performance. There has been a move away from ratings, whether single or multiple, to agreed statements that are oriented to behaviour and future improvement. Another trend, although still confined to a relatively small minority of organisations, is towards 360 degree feedback, which involves collecting performance data on individuals from a range of sources, including immediate superiors and subordinates, peers and both internal and external customers. The concept of the 'balanced scorecard', which brings together customer orientation, financial perspective, internal operational aspects and innovative or developmental dimensions, has become popular at both organisational and lower levels as a result. It also helps to reconcile the competing interests of different stakeholders.

Applying these ideas to your own experience

How does your organisation approach the issues in measuring performance? How do you do it in your own area of responsibility?

In considering what measures to use, certain guidelines should be borne in mind:

- they should be output measures not input measures
- there needs to be a unit of measurement
- the measures should be objective and observable
- the results must be within the jobholder's control
- existing measures should be used where feasible.

Stage 4 – review

The final stage in most performance management cycles is the performance review, although many people, including most employees, see it as the primary and most important aspect of the cycle. The review is designed to allow both parties to the process to consider how achievements have met the goals set during the planning stage. A review looks at results, both tangible and intangible, and provides the springboard for determining where to concentrate efforts as the cycle returns to the planning stage. Reviewing performance typically has three components:

- regular informal meetings
- interim formal reviews
- annual appraisal.

Performance management will not work very well if it is only seen as an annual process. The performance management cycle works best if it is used as a series of mini-cycles, throughout the year with continuing feedback. Then, when it comes to a more detailed review and planning session, there should be no surprises. Regular performance review keeps you in constant touch with what is happening, and helps build a more effective performance management process.

Peter knew that he had been lucky to be given the job. The job description had been just what he had been looking for and it gave him a good outline of his role. But as time went on he realised that something was missing. Although he felt that he was doing a good job, there seemed to be no easy way to demonstrate this, either to his boss or even to himself. He needed some way of measuring himself against the requirements of the job, and he became concerned that his boss didn't seem to have any way of doing this either, so that he began to feel that he was not being properly appreciated.

In conducting a performance review session, it is desirable to have allowed the employee to have engaged in preliminary self-assessment. This involves the employee more directly and is likely to produce a less defensive response. Indeed, it is desirable to let the individual do most of the talking, leaving the manager to listen actively for nuances in what is being said, as well as watching for body language. It is also important to recognise achievements. Whilst there are arguments against having forms which must be filled in, thereby adding a bureaucratic element to what should be personal rather than impersonal, a form does help to provide focus and a level of consistency.

The review process incorporates a very important part of the total cycle, namely appraisal, which is significant enough to justify separate attention. In addition, rewards – another separate topic – may also be part of the review process.

Appraisal systems

Performance management, to be effective, requires a direct interaction between the management and the workforce, and for most purposes a system of appraisal provides this. There are a number of reasons why appraisal is necessary from the viewpoints of the organisation, the manager and the employee.

The organisation benefits from:

- standard information about its employees
- the facility to develop individuals based on appraisal information
- being able to plan its human resource needs more accurately.

The manager benefits from:

- objective guidelines for assessing staff
- gaining a better understanding of staff needs
- improved relationships with staff.

The individual benefits from:

- an opportunity to discuss his or her work objectively
- the ability to evaluate performance
- consideration of future training and development needs
- improved relationships with his or her manager.

Any organisation needs to know the strengths and weaknesses of its employees; any manager needs this information about the people who work in his or her department; and any individual needs to know how he or she is performing. A good appraisal scheme can satisfy all these needs. We have also talked about the desirability of a PDP, which acts as the employee's personal record.

An appraisal interview is a formal occasion, but the manager should try to make the employee feel as much at ease as possible, allowing sufficient time and not allowing any interruptions. Adequate notice should be given to allow for any preparation.

Employees should have written down how well they think they have done, including how far they have met their objectives, in relation to both performance and development, and this should be discussed, preferably with strengths being taken before weaknesses. The employee should be encouraged to suggest a resolution of any weaknesses. The appraisal interview is not the place to raise serious issues of under-performance for the first time. The objective is to try to achieve an agreed conclusion about the rating of performance, and especially if this involves decisions with implications for pay. A rating would normally relate to a category such as excellent, standard or unsatisfactory, or a numerical scale of some sort.

Following the review of performance it is time to discuss plans for the following year, as a new cycle starts. This includes future objectives and any development needs, and these may include longer-term aspects of the employee's position in the organisation.

Any agreement should be recorded for use in the next cycle, whilst if there are disagreements the employee should be made aware of how to appeal against a decision. In many organisations, reports also need to be countersigned by a senior manager to provide consistency.

An obvious issue for appraisal concerns what to do about under-performance, whether in the appraisal situation or at some other time. Any problem should be identified as early as possible in the cycle through regular feedback, and support and coaching should be available. But when performance consistently fails to reach expectations, managers must be prepared to face up to the issue and should have been trained in how to handle it. If this is still not sufficient, disciplinary action may be necessary, with the first formal stage being a written warning identifying the problem and what is required to resolve it. This is an issue which is taken up in the following two chapters.

An appraisal system helps you as a manager to learn more about your employees, their problems and needs and how their aspirations are being fulfilled by their job. It can help you to increase their motivation by discovering the satisfying and less satisfying aspects of their jobs in the opinion of the individuals who perform them. It can help to improve individual performance and productivity and, thus, increase your job satisfaction as the person accountable for your area of responsibility.

Randell (1984) suggests that an appraisal system should have some – but not, necessarily, all – of the following purposes:

- Evaluation – to enable the organisation to share out financial and other rewards apparently 'fairly'.
- Auditing – to discover the work potential, both present and future, of individuals and departments.
- Constructing succession plans – for human resource departmental and corporate planning purposes.
- Discovering training needs – by exposing inadequacies and deficiencies that could be remedied through training.

- Motivating staff – to reach organisational standards and objectives.
- Developing individuals – by offering advice, information, praise or sanctions.
- Improving standards – and thus performance.
- Checking the effectiveness – of personnel procedures and practices.

There are, however, some potentially negative aspects of an appraisal:

- It can be stressful for both sides and, if not handled properly, disruptive of the relationship between them.
- Although mutual trust is desirable, it will not always be present.
- The converse of this is that the desire to avoid stress can lead to over-ranking when judged objectively.
- It can be seen as a 'tick box' process, about putting people into boxes.
- Subjective evaluations are almost unavoidable.

Applying these ideas to your own experience

If you currently operate an appraisal system in your organisation, which of the above purposes does it fulfil? And is it subject to any of the negative dimensions?

If you do not have a formal appraisal system, how do you and your organisation fulfil any of the functions above? Is this satisfactory?

In a formal appraisal system, there needs to be an assessment of the individual's performance over a period of time. Self-assessment by the individual is one way of measuring this, as is peer assessment or your own evaluation of how a person is performing in their current job. However, objective measures of performance are preferable and much fairer to the individual. Has he or she achieved an overall, agreed standard of performance against criteria which were known in advance? The job description is an obvious point of reference here, providing it is up to date and, if possible, includes performance measures or, if the team has set itself objectives which can be measured, the individual can be assessed against these. Unless the individual is actually aware of the standards against which he or she is being measured, the appraisal is unfair and invalid.

Having agreed the objectives and measured the individual against these, that person's strengths and weaknesses in relation to the criteria can be identified. Ideally, these should be set down in writing or on a special appraisal form in agreement with the person being appraised. Thereafter, the appraiser and the person being appraised should discuss and agree (a) what specific learning and development the individual needs to remedy weak areas and (b) what his or her objectives should be over the period before the next appraisal or interim review. An interim review is often necessary since most formal appraisals are carried out on an annual basis. Such reviews serve to monitor progress towards the next set of objectives.

The manager needs to establish a relationship of trust with the individual and all appraisal discussions and records should be confidential between those two. In some organisations it is customary for a summary of the appraisal, agreed with the individual, to contribute towards promotion, regrading or salary review processes: in others, the full appraisal record is used. It is essential, in these cases, that the individual has seen the appraisal summary or report before it goes further.

We all engage in appraisal on an everyday basis, particularly with people we know well and within our own close domestic circle. We make judgements about whether people are performing above or below our expectations. We comment to others on the performance of the public transport system, the state of the roads, the content of television programmes, the performance of our bosses and subordinates, the way our children behave, the actions of government and the law and so on. Yet, in Western cultures, we hesitate to tell most people about their weaknesses to their faces and, for many people, it is difficult for them to praise people directly as well.

The 'praise sandwich' has long been a cornerstone of giving feedback – praising the subordinate at the outset for good performance, followed by a constructive discussion of areas of weakness and concluding with a restatement of his or her strengths. An appraisal that concentrates almost solely on areas of poor performance will result in the person being appraised feeling resentful and poorly motivated to improve, and this is certainly not the object of the exercise.

Gil knew he had a difficult time ahead when it came to appraising Andy. The man just wasn't up to the job and his team were performing less well than any of the others – they never seemed to produce results. He had had to make a presentation to the board earlier in the year and, by all accounts, it had been disastrous.

Andy was defensive, 'It's all this extra work I'm expected to do,' he complained, 'it doesn't leave me enough time. And everyone else in my team has been here longer than me and knows what they're doing.' Through careful questioning, Gil discovered that the sales manager had asked Andy to prepare a detailed sales plan for the department, which Gil knew nothing about. He also realised that Andy had not been given any induction when he joined the company and that, when he had asked to be sent on a course to improve his presentation skills, Gil's assistant had turned this down. Much of Andy's poor performance was not his own fault.

Carly was dreading her annual appraisal. She knew that the parents of two of the children in her class had objected formally about how much homework she was giving out and that, despite all her efforts, the end-of-term show had been poorly organised. Her Junior Choir had excelled itself at the festival but, on the other hand, class work was a bit behind and she was always late with her reports.

She was pleasantly surprised when Miss Bowles praised her not only about the choir's success but also about her work with two children with learning difficulties, and felt relaxed enough to admit her own shortcomings in other parts of her job. She agreed that she had taken on too much and set her targets too high initially and that she needed to prioritise her work and manage her time better. Together they agreed on her objectives for the following year, with interim objectives which Miss Bowles would review with her at the end of each term. Carly also agreed to attend a time management course, which was being run locally – she wished she'd known about this before. She left her appraisal with a sense of relief that they had been able to discuss her weak areas objectively and identify ways of improvement in these and she was buoyed up by the recognition of what she had done well.

Applying these ideas to your own experience

How often have you given feedback to your employees outside the appraisal process?

Managing rewards

Rewards are central to work and the employment relationship and are the key quid pro quo that workers receive for their efforts, as well as having a major effect on morale and efficiency. There are many different types of payment systems, but the two main categories are basic pay for the hour, week or year, usually according to an organisational or national pay scale, and those in which pay is dependent on performance, whether at an individual or group level. This latter is sometimes known as the effort bargain, and the assumptions lying behind payment by results systems are that workers can be induced to provide more effort.

Clearly pay can be an important factor in managing performance, both directly as a reward for performance, or indirectly that without some element of reward the performance management cycle can be seen as lacking relevance. 63 per cent of

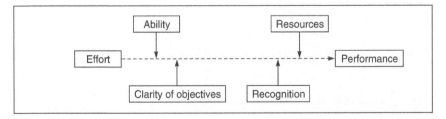

Figure 7.3 Factors linking effort and performance

appraisals were not linked directly to pay in the 2011 *Workplace Employment Relations Study* (van Woonroy and others 2013), but the trend is nevertheless upwards and in financial services it was 68 per cent in the 2011 study. There are also considerable disadvantages in linking pay to performance, notably that in a team, success is not just dependent on the individual and indeed the individual's contribution may be difficult to measure. Moreover, it has been found with payment by results systems that employees soon learn to focus on those parts of the job that affect pay whilst ignoring those that don't, for instance working collaboratively. In addition, measured results are from the past, whilst the desire may be to focus on the future. Furthermore, employees may be less willing to admit weaknesses at their appraisal if they think it is going to affect their pay.

However, it is too easy to think of pay as the sole focus of rewards to the exclusion of other aspects of rewards at work, which can be both intrinsic and extrinsic, as noted below:

Intrinsic rewards

- self-respect
- sense of achievement
- feeling of having learned something
- feeling of having contributed to a team or wider effort
- self-fulfilment.

Extrinsic rewards

- developing individuals – by offering advice, information, praise or sanctions
- improving standards – and thus performance
- checking the effectiveness – of personnel procedures and practices
- pay
- fringe benefits – holidays, pensions, sick pay etc
- pleasant working conditions
- personal development
- promotion and career opportunities
- variety and challenge of work
- status within organisation
- status outside organisation
- praise
- friendship.

Moreover, some rewards can be communal as well as individual.

Applying these ideas to your own experience

How do you rank the above rewards in terms of your own priorities? What do you think the priorities of those working for you would be?

Different people will have different attitudes to different parts of the range of rewards. Some people, who are highly instrumental, will want to maximise their direct earnings and little else. Others see pay as secondary to the self-esteem and social opportunities they see work as providing. Others again will focus on non-work aspects of life and want work to interfere with these as little as possible. Workers can also be in quite different situations, with some being in stable, core jobs, and others being in much less stable peripheral positions, and this too will influence their attitudes towards an optimum set of rewards. Employees will see rewards as a key indicator of whether the employer is treating them fairly and transparently in relation both to the work they do and also as compared to other workers. The job of the manager is to understand how different aspects of rewards are valued by the employees, with a view to maximising both their mix of rewards and the efficiencies which the employer is seeking. But the manager must also cope with individual differences in the valuation of the reward, and also changes over time in the way rewards are perceived. Few reward systems are capable of producing optimal results indefinitely, and most need reviewing regularly. This is particularly true of payment systems.

From the company's perspective, it needs to provide rewards that meet a number of objectives:

- add value to the organisation, bearing in mind that personnel costs are typically more than half and often much more than half of total organisational costs
- support the main strategic objectives of efficiency, quality, teamwork and customer orientation
- relate to external market factors, but not to the exclusion of internal dimensions
- obtain a suitably skilled and efficient labour force
- communicate the organisation's expectations of performance and standards
- is integrated with other HR policies
- has some contribution from line managers to permit a devolved implementation of performance management
- is comprehensible, equitable and transparent in its operation
- encourages appropriate behaviour in relation to the organisation's goals.

All reward systems have trade-offs between different objectives, both for the employer and the employee, whilst it is also quite possible that collective bargaining with trade unions will be an influential determinant of both objectives and outcomes. Moreover, rewards are a matter of market as well as performance or job factors. Broadly speaking, the bargaining power of unskilled and semi-skilled workers in the labour market has declined, especially where such skills can be substituted by technology or lower paid workers in other countries. On the other hand, the power of certain types of knowledge workers who hold key aspects of intellectual capital in their heads and can take the assets of the organisation with them when they leave the building has increased very considerably. These factors are primarily to do with the nature of external labour markets, but there are also internal factors in which individual contributions can be taken into account.

What can front-line managers contribute to the rewards system, other than the evaluation provided through the appraisal system? Following the global financial crisis of 2007–2008 real wages declined in Britain as inflation rose faster than wages, whilst higher unemployment heightened employee uncertainty. This raises the question of whether there is an alternative system of rewards for people whose morale might have suffered. Wage structures are likely to be set at the organisation level, so what can the front-line manager do for his or her staff? There are actually several possibilities for the front-line manager:

- be positive yourself
- emphasise togetherness, even if only 'we're all in this together'
- end the blame game
- learn from your staff and pursue their suggestions
- promote enthusiasm and pride rather than solely efficiency
- take an interest in your staff and their families
- recognition, giving praise and thanks where it is justified
- development to improve skills
- flexibility in the timing of work
- trying to reduce stress and insecurity.

Problems and successes of performance management

If the performance management cycle sounds very attractive, it needs to be noted that it is much harder to implement these principles and achieve the desired outcomes than it is to state them, and it is also easy to identify a list of potential problems. The ability of front-line managers to play their role effectively can make an important contribution, particularly in providing coaching support and making good decisions about reward. They in turn however need training and support to enable them to carry out these responsibilities effectively. Difficulties can arise when they are not provided with adequate training or where new systems are introduced too quickly (IPM 1992).

Another common reason for difficulty is that schemes are often imposed from above and do not give people, or even middle and junior managers, a sense of ownership in how they develop. Thus, McKevitt and Lawton (1996), in studying performance management in the public sector, noted as their central finding that: 'the lack of attention paid to middle and junior management in the development and implementation of performance measurement systems and hence a lack of embeddedness of systems throughout the organisation'. Inadequate account of the prevailing culture is yet another reason for problems.

Both of these latter two reasons imply that organisations assume a unitary view, namely that employers and employees share common interests, instead of a pluralist perspective that tries to recognise potential conflicts of interest. Some of its other potential problems are: frequent modifications; poor communication; over-complexity, with too much paperwork a particular problem; goals which are too ambitious; and lack of support and training for the front-line managers who enact the policy intentions.

Performance management, it appears, is not working as well as it should (Brown 2011). HR departments have set themselves an ambitious agenda to marry organisational purpose and goals with individual actions and performance, business direction with employee communications and engagement, sophisticated assessment techniques and multiple information sources, and linking the disparate strands of HR practice: talent management, development, reward and diversity. It all sounds fine, but concerns remain about the skills and attitudes of reviewing managers, the consistency and quality of approach across large organisations, the complexity of the paperwork and the value of outputs. If it has all become too complex to be workable, what should be done?

Performance management has proved a particular flashpoint at HMRC, where dissatisfaction over a new appraisal system caused employees to walk out in February. The Association of Revenue and Customs president, Tony Wallace, said the new system forces managers to identify 10 per cent of the workforce as 'must improve' against performance goals. 'The evidence we're hearing from our members is that it is designed to find the 10 per cent rather than give a proper assessment of people's performance in their jobs.' *People Management* (June 2014), p. 9.

Thus, performance management is sometimes seen as a system which promises more than it delivers, with a big gap between aspirations and reality. Nevertheless, the basic underpinning of performance management around the appraisal system is generally accepted as one of the most important influences on employee and organisational performance. It tends to be what is put on top of the basic structure and how the process is operated that creates the problems.

Gillian Quinton at Buckinghamshire County Council says that when she introduced a new performance management system to link pay and perform- ance more closely, she initially faced union objections. However, more than 80 per cent of staff eventually signed up voluntarily. Communication, she says, is key. She points to training and managers' soft skills around difficult conversations as crucial to ensuring that the system does not fall into disre- pute. *People Management* (June 2014), p. 9.

In addition Brown (2011) provides a couple of examples where perform- ance management can be effective. A report on the influence of HR practices on hospital mortality rates found that a hospital which appraises about 20 per cent more staff and trains about 20 per cent more appraisers is likely to have 1,090 fewer deaths for every 100,000 admissions. In Tesco, the Steering Wheel consists of four quadrants – customers, operations, finance and people – setting key performance indicators for each, which underpin how its stores operate and has been seen as a key factor in the company's growth.

Activities

1. Draw up a list of the different ways in which your organisation measures people's performance.
2. Either suggest improvements to an existing appraisal system in your own organisation or design an appraisal system which would meet the objectives outlined in this chapter.
3. Identify the training needs for individuals within your area of responsibility. What provision for development could you provide from within the organisation?
4. Identify the objectives which your organisation reflects in its rewards system.

References

Acas, (2014) *How to Manage Performance*. Advisory booklet. London, Acas.
Brown D., (2011) 'Performance management: fine intentions', *People Management*, September.
IPM, (1992) *Performance Management in the UK: An Analysis of the Issues*. London, Institute of Personnel Management.
McKevitt D. and Lawton A., (1996) 'The Manager, the citizen, the politician and performance measures', *Public Money and Management* (July–September), 49–54.
People Management (June 2014), 9.
Purcell J. and Hutchinson S., (2007) 'Front-line managers as agents in the HRM-performance causal chain: theory, analysis and evidence', *Human Resource Management Journal* 17(1), 3–20.
Randell G., (1984) *Staff Appraisal*. London, Institute of Personnel and Development,.
van Wanrooy B., Bewley H., Bryson A., Forth J., Freeth S., Stokes L. and Wood S., (2013) *Employment Relations in the Shadow of Recession: Findings from the 2011 Workplace Employment Relations Study*. Basingstoke, Palgrave Macmillan.

8 Managing challenging situations

Introduction

This chapter moves away from the core roles of the front-line manager, by introducing some potentially problematic issues for managers in which their assumptions of relative predictability and control may need to be modified and they may need to respond to situations rather than creating them. They can be some of the most difficult issues facing a front-line manager who has often been trained to deal with the specific tasks relating to his or her job and feels ill-equipped to deal with complex problems not directly related to the job function.

Nevertheless many complaints at employment tribunals arise through poor communication and genuine misunderstandings at the departmental level. Thus it is important that front-line managers are able to recognise issues and know where to seek help if necessary. There are two main clusters of challenging areas: one dealing with the dynamics of organisational life such as power, conflict and stress; and the other dealing with the institutionalisation of issues such as grievances and discipline and ultimately dismissal. There are some very helpful guides available online from Acas on many of these issues at www.acas.org.uk.

The following topics are dealt with in this chapter:

- managing power
- bullying and harassment
- avoiding stress
- holding difficult conversations
- managing conflict
- dealing with unions
- managing grievances
- managing discipline
- dismissal.

We start with the first cluster of problematic issues in managing people, namely the dynamics of organisational life, dealing with the management of power, bullying and harassment, stress and conflict.

Managing power

(handwritten margin notes: "Hierarchical cue page" and "gain → power / How to gain → power")

Power is a necessity in organisations if objectives are to be achieved because it gives a focus to the social system that exists in the organisation or the unit within it. Managers need power to do their jobs effectively, and they need to know what creates power and how to use it. Power is the capacity to affect other people's behaviour without their consent, and is a personal attribute which has an effect on others. However, managers need not be the only focus of power in units; individuals or groups may be able to exercise power formally or informally. So what are the sources of power in an organisation?

- Authority is defined in terms of the hierarchy and structure of the organisation and is dependent on its resources. It gives the right to control finance, people, information etc, but it is only legitimated if others recognise and concede it. Authority is therefore limited, and does not guarantee power, although it is obviously an important source of power.
- Physical characteristics, including intelligence and physical presence.
- Personality, which involves both emotional dimensions and behaviour, and can provide charisma, which is a high level of ability to influence people through personality.
- Achievements and reputation.
- Action in groups as opposed to individuals.
- Rewards, such as the capacity to reward people financially or psychologically.
- The obverse of this, the power to punish or criticise, can also be an important source of power.
- Access to important people elsewhere, but usually higher up in the organisation, or outside of it.
- Access to resources, especially information.
- Interpersonal, political and social skills.
- Wealth.
- Expertise, based on knowledge, skill or experience.

Power is also endemic to the employer–employee relationship and has been a source of controversy throughout history. At the time of writing (July 2014), an example of this is zero-hours contracts, a topic which is being consulted on by the government. The Acas contribution said that exclusivity clauses with no guarantee of work were bad for both sides, creating insecurity for employees and undermining trust in the employment relationship. It is not only contractual exclusivity that can be damaging. Acas research found that many zero-hours workers were afraid to look for work elsewhere, turn down hours, question their rights and entitlements, or raise a grievance in case offers of work are withdrawn or 'zeroed down' in response. This amounted, it said, to 'effective exclusivity', just as corrosive as anything written in a contract. It reflected the power imbalance in the employment relationship and contributed to a sense of ill-treatment felt by many zero-hours workers – particularly when they had been working for their employers for many years, or had an emotional commitment to the people they were dealing with, as in the caring and teaching professions (Acas Newsletter, April 2014).

Power games are, however, likely to be part of organisational life, and managers must be aware of their implications if they are to be effective. But power games in organisations can be damaging to their effectiveness. Moreover, others – either individuals or groups – in your area of responsibility may also have some of the attributes of power noted above, so there may be alternative locations for the exercise of power. Indeed, it is likely that there are several alternative sources of power in the different interest groups in the unit, and conflict may be the outcome, as noted below.

Moreover, because power depends to a considerable extent on the legitimation of others, this can be withdrawn if the manager does something which is unacceptable to the group and his power will have been diminished. Perhaps, equally importantly, their respect for him may have been diminished, and respect is a key dimension of legitimation. Managers therefore need to be aware of the limits of their legitimated power. They need to use political skills and other sources of power, as well as authority, to influence behaviour. Authority alone is unlikely to be a source of effective power for very long. An ability to understand what is going on around you and being aware of other people's emotions – empathy, in a word – is more likely to bring success.

Office politics are often seen as a disorganised way of expressing power. Although almost universally disparaged, they continue to flourish. So what are the tips for avoiding their excesses?

- avoid gossiping yourself; don't say anything you wouldn't put into a general email
- but take time to listen and observe, especially in a new job
- don't alienate anyone and 'keep your enemies close'
- get to know everyone and don't align yourself with particular groups
- be prepared to stand up for yourself if need be.

Applying these ideas to your own experience

What are the sources of power in your unit? How concentrated is it? How can you respond to it? How does 'office politics' manifest itself in your context?

Bullying and harassment

A Chartered Institute of Personnel and Development study found that 15 per cent of employees had experienced bullying or harassment in the preceding two years, and another 33 per cent said they had witnessed it (*People Management* October 2013, 26). As the article noted: 'few organisations seem to have got to grips with how to handle it.' Clearly, both bullying and harassment are bad news in the workplace, creating poor morale and productivity and damaging to the reputations of both individuals and the organisation. However, most of the miscreants are unaware that they are bullying, which makes it even more of a problem.

Janette Hirst says she worked in the college's electrical installation section for just over 12 years but the career she had worked so hard for slipped away from her following a change of management during the second half of 2010. The 44-year-old said she was not the only member of the team who allegedly encountered an intimidating and bullying atmosphere. In a written statement presented to an employment tribunal, she said: 'I became increasingly unhappy with the Curriculum Team Leader's unacceptable management style during 2011.' Janette has been awarded more than £78,000 after successfully pursuing a claim for unfair dismissal (Acas Newsletter, March 2014).

Bullying may be described as 'offensive, intimidating, malicious or insulting behaviour, an abuse or misuse of power through means that undermine, humiliate, denigrate or injure the recipient', whilst harassment, as defined by the Equality Act 2010, is 'unwanted conduct related to a relevant protected characteristic, which has the purpose or effect of violating an individual's dignity or creating an intimidating, hostile, degrading or offensive environment for that individual' (Acas 2014a). Nevertheless, in spite of these apparently clear definitions, the two terms are not always easy to recognise in practice, with grey areas of definition or perhaps operating insidiously so as to be unclear to outsiders, and leading to accusations of overreaction. One person's strong management can be seen as bullying by another. Managers should be prepared to look out for issues of such behaviour, rather than just waiting for complaints.

There are several steps that can be taken to handle these problems:

- A policy framework with examples and a statement that they may lead to disciplinary action.
- A good example by managers, remembering that 'strong' management may sometimes be seen to tip over into bullying behaviour.
- Prompt dealing with any issues, with confidentiality for complainants, and an objective and independent investigation.

- Mediation, used by, amongst others, East Sussex County Council and the Rank Group, in which the focus is to look to the future, rather than dwell on what has gone wrong.
- Disciplinary action.

For further advice on this topic, visit the National Bullying Helpline website www. nationalbullyinghelpline.co.uk.

Avoiding stress

In Chapter 2 we looked at your concerns with personal stress; here, we examine stress within the organisation. Stress is everywhere: students have examination stress; soldiers have battle stress; many families suffer stress. But most of all, stress is a feature of organisational life: most managers are likely to find themselves facing stress as an issue in their organisation; if they do not they are either very good managers or exceptionally lucky. People at the top are not immune; Sir Hector Sants took leave of absence from his role as Head of Global Compliance at Barclays Bank in October 2013 because of 'exhaustion and stress' (Tovey 2013). Many others would not dare to admit it. Moreover, the implications of stress can be very significant personally, organisationally, legally and financially. At the level of the economy, stress is estimated to cost 12.8 million days lost or, in monetary terms, £3.7b a year and affects one in five of us (Janes 2013). And it is not only direct losses of days or money: about 40 per cent of staff turnover is said to be due to stress, and many of the inefficiencies of people's daily activities can also be associated with stress. Frequently work is not the only factor, and sources of stress can be brought into work by domestic or community issues. However, work is still arguably the key source and is often associated with interpersonal aspects of the work situation, with 'the boss from hell' often seen as the key culprit.

So what is stress? The Health and Safety Executive defines stress as 'The reaction people have to excessive pressures or other types of demand placed on them. It arises when they worry they can't cope.' However, having too little to do or lack of any variety in one's work can also cause stress by creating boredom and dissatisfaction. Some pressure is necessary for optimum performance, and it is obviously difficult to get the balance right. How people cope with stress depends on their personality, their ability to accept change and their tolerance of ambiguity. Some people thrive in stressful situations, as is often said of high achievers and of top sportsmen or women, whilst others cannot cope.

Stress is not just caused by managers, but lies deeper in the organisational context or culture. Research by the industrial psychologist Peter Warr (1987) has identified nine features of jobs which influence stress. These are:

- low job discretion, ie little freedom to make decisions or to exercise control over work
- low use of skills
- low or high work demands

- low task variety, ie repetitive, monotonous work
- high uncertainty about how well or poorly you are performing and about the survival of the company and your place in it
- low pay, creating difficult financial circumstances
- poor working conditions, especially noisy, hot, wet or dangerous environments
- low interpersonal support at work
- carrying out a job which is perceived as being of low value in society.

In isolation, any one of these features is unlikely to cause severe stress. Rather, it is the combination of factors which lead to this condition. In particular, Warr found that high work demands combined with low job discretion was particularly stressful. To this list above might be added the long hours culture of much of British industry by which British workers spend more hours per day at work than their Continental counterparts, with one in six working more than 48 hours a week.

Applying these ideas to your own experience

Do any of these conditions apply in your unit? What might be done about them? How might you respond if they cannot be changed?

The first step in coping with stress is to recognise that it exists. Stress is now accepted as a physiological response which can become an illness, and some of the wide range of the body's reactions to stress were provided in Chapter 2. Some aspects of stress can be minimised through improved job design (see Chapter 4), whereas others require medical help. Work-related stress is an illness and should be treated as such; it is not a weakness. The longer it is allowed to go untreated, the longer it may take for the individual to recover, so you are not doing yourself or your organisation any favours by ignoring the symptoms.

How to manage stress is largely about avoiding it rather than dealing with its consequences. The most important factor in avoiding stress lies in the nature of the organisation itself in providing an open, dynamic environment with a clear sense of direction. But there are also a number of specific ways that can be introduced by the individual manager providing leadership in a problematic situation:

- using a people-oriented management style
- putting people in jobs which are within their capabilities
- re-evaluating people's motivation and not placing too many demands on them
- redesigning jobs to make them more acceptable, in particular by removing ambiguities or conflict in the role or by increasing the amount of autonomy that workers have

- counselling people to enable them to talk about their problems, either with a mentor or with a member of the personnel department. Medical attention may be necessary in some circumstances
- giving workers better training to enable them to do the job better; this may also go for managers, for whom training may enable them to see the needs of their staff
- appraisal or other performance reviews which allow a dialogue between the manager and the worker about their performance and any problems with it
- examining the work–life balance of employees.

Ideally, the intention is to build up in people a resilience based on self-awareness and self-esteem, which breeds a positive outlook towards life and which in turn enables them to tolerate more stress. At the same time, of course, the organisation needs to work to reduce the causes of stress.

For further advice, see www.stress-busting.co.uk and also www.hse.gov.uk.

Holding difficult conversations

Every manager will have to face up to holding a difficult conversation at some time, sometimes unexpectedly at short notice or relating to issues which ostensibly have little to do with the immediate work situation. Some will have elements of a grievance, even if not specifically designated as such. However, if at all possible, managers should prepare for the meeting, checking organisational policies and procedures and seeking help if necessary. Indeed, a key preliminary issue may be whether your level is the appropriate place at which to handle the problem, and whether it should be sent to a higher level. But accepting it, a first objective is to contain the problem and to look to the future, whilst a second consideration is how formal or informal the process should be. An informal approach is more likely to lead to a resolution, but some issues may need a formal approach from the start.

During the conversation, there are some key steps:

- setting the right tone to start with
- clarifying the issue and the purpose of the meeting
- reassure about confidentiality
- ask for an explanation
- the need to stay in control
- keep the issue to the matter in hand
- focus on the issue not the person
- think on the spot
- meaningful communication on both sides is essential
- for the manager it is a time for 'active' listening
- be prepared to negotiate
- try to agree a way forward
- don't let the meeting ramble on.

Managing conflict

[handwritten: During feedbk session - constructive conflict]

Conflict is generally accepted as an inevitable part of organisational life; indeed, Thomas (2002: 3) has estimated that managers spend about a quarter of their time handling conflicts of one sort or another. The term brings with it connotations of antagonism and undesirability; however, it should not automatically be thought that all conflict is dysfunctional. Constructive conflict can introduce new solutions to a problem, define power relationships within a group, bring non-rational emotional dimensions into the open and provide for the release of catharsis by identifying long-established conflict. On the other hand, destructive conflict can result in a loss of the main objectives in the pursuit of sub-group interests, induce people to be defensive and eventually result in the disintegration of the group. Handled well, things improve; handled badly, they can deteriorate to a point where external authority or advice needs to be brought in, and no manager welcomes this because it reflects on his or her own position.

Sources of conflict are endemic in organisations and whilst some can be superficial, many go very deep into our personal identity:

- Interpersonal differences. For all kinds of reasons, some people don't get on with others – you can't expect to like everyone you meet or work with, nor to be liked by everyone else. There are differences in personality, temperament, outlook and beliefs which make this impossible.
- Misunderstandings. These can arise because of different languages or accents or simply because people genuinely didn't understand what was said or implied.
- Differences in values and beliefs. Values and beliefs are shaped by experience and upbringing and, thus, are likely to differ considerably and are usually deeply rooted and difficult to change; they need to be recognised and respected if conflict is to be avoided. Being a member of a group gives people identity and self-esteem and makes them feel different to other groups.
- Differences in interest. When a conflict arises, it is common to find that people have different interests in its resolution – or in its continuation. Interests may be personal or departmental, but they are likely to centre on competition of an economic nature.

These differences between groups or individuals have effects which are perceptual, emotional and behavioural. The perceptions created by group identification will be exacerbated by group competition. At the emotional level, emotions relative to the other group are likely to be negative, creating an 'us' against 'them' situation.

So what does the manager do in these circumstances, which are likely to be fairly frequent and in some cases ongoing? None of the actions is without its own problems.

[handwritten: Understand not a competition — win-win situation]

Try to ensure that both sides of a conflict gain by cooperation rather than having a competition where one side wins and the other loses. This may not be easy because of the psychological factors, but it will at least reduce the tension.

- Provide open communication between and with the groups, if necessary with the manager acting as a mediator, to identify the issues and clarify the organisational objectives. Again, this may be easier said than done, but it should at least be tried.
- Use power to resolve conflict. This may have the advantage of being relatively quick, but it also carries the potential for resentment and an ongoing unsatisfactory situation.
- Build trust. This is the most desirable way to resolve the problems, but as the longevity of ethnic, religious and class feuds around the world reminds us, it is often very difficult to achieve. Trust takes a long time to establish, and requires open communication as a prerequisite.
- Problem solving through negotiation. Most situations are not in fact zero sum, ie where if one side gains, the other side loses an equal amount. Most situations can be turned with careful thought to one where both sides can gain something, even if one gains more than the other. This will also probably involve compromise, a key dimension of successful negotiation.

Another way of considering how to respond to conflict is the Thomas-Kilmann Conflict Mode Instrument (Thomas 2002), which identifies five modes of response, each with a different set of trade-offs, behavioural skills and contexts suitable for its effective use:

- competing – seeking to impose a decision
- collaborating – reconciling interests with a win-win outcome
- compromising – looking for a half-way solution
- avoiding – trying to avoid the conflict situation
- accommodating – conceding your interests to the opponent.

Applying these ideas to your own experience

Think about a conflict at work. Which of the above sources do you think was at the root of the conflict? What was the most appropriate means of resolving it?

We now move to the second cluster of problem areas, that of providing structures and procedures to deal with disagreements at work. Having sensible institutions and procedures which are understood and trusted by all concerned is arguably the best safeguard against the escalation of a minor incident into a serious problem.

Dealing with unions

There is still a residual view that unions are anti-capitalist and anti-managerial, striving to overturn the existing economic system. This has never been true other than in a miniscule percentage of union membership, but it is even less true now. Over the last 30 years, British unions have lost power and membership – in 1979 membership was 13 million, by 2012 it had fallen to 6.5 million – and have also become much concerned with two broad objectives: working with management collectively to improve standards and efficiency, and helping their members as individuals through a range of advisory services. A survey carried out for the TUC found that people did not want an adversarial relationship with their employer. More than 70 per cent of both members and non-members preferred the statement 'We work with management to improve the workplace and working conditions' to an alternative 'We defend workers against unfair treatment by management'.

A good company recognises that it needs to hear the voice of its workforce and in many cases a union is best placed to provide this. Nevertheless, the decline of unions in the last 30 years, especially in the private sector, has also seen a rise in the interaction with workers as individuals rather than as members of groups, and a growing use of the term 'employee relations' to replace the older collective term of 'industrial relations'. Nevertheless, there are still instances in the private sector with complex union relationships: easyJet, the low-cost airline, was dealing with 15 unions and 6 representative bodies in 2013 (easyJet 2013).

Industrial relations can be seen as a system of institutions, rules and procedures, and both formal and informal processes, by which the regulation of employment through collective bargaining and conflict resolution takes place. A formal set of written agreements may well be complemented by the climate of relationships between the parties and elements of custom and practice whose origins might be lost in the mists of time. Much of the history of British industry in the last century was determined in considerable part by major issues of industrial relations, such as the extent of managerial control or 'right to manage', the introduction of new working practices and conflicts over wage levels. We will not go into industrial relations at length, because it is likely to be operated at organisational or even national level, and also because a discussion of its institutions will not be directly applicable to many managers. Instead, we will concentrate on the implications of two dimensions of dealing with your employees with which you are very likely to have to deal, namely the management of grievances and discipline.

Applying these ideas to your own experience

What is the structure of industrial relations in your organisation? If there are no unions, is there any other mechanism through which employees can express themselves collectively?

Managing grievances

A grievance begins as an expression of dissatisfaction by an individual or group of employees in respect of 'any measure or situation which directly affects or may affect the conditions of employment of one or several workers in the undertaking when that measure or situation appears contrary to the provisions of an applicable collective agreement or of an individual contract of employment, to work rules, to laws or regulations or to the custom or usage of the occupation or country' (International Labour Organization 1965). A grievance may arise within an industrial relations structure in which there are shop stewards, union branches and full-time officials. Or it may arise in a context where there is no system of worker representation and individuals are acting on their own. Or there may be some intermediate situation. The potential for grievances exists irrespective of the institutional background.

A grievance usually starts with some kind of trigger in the form of management or peer action, which gives rise to individual or group dissatisfaction. If the dissatisfaction is initially experienced by an individual, the person may seek allies to support him or her in their opinions or may go to his or her manager and voice the dissatisfaction. At this stage, it may be no more than a 'dissatisfaction' with some aspect of the individual's working environment, which can be handled sensitively and the dissatisfaction reduced or eliminated if it is within the manager's control. If the dissatisfaction is more widespread, the kind of informal group cohesion described in Chapter 6 can occur and the discontent can grow accordingly. As a manager, you can often prevent conflict from escalating by becoming aware of it at an early stage and trying to resolve it before it becomes a formal grievance.

The Advisory, Conciliation and Arbitration Service (Acas) in its Advisory Handbook *Discipline and Grievances at Work* (2014b) has provided guidance that employers should consider when handling a grievance:

- Deal with grievances informally if possible – a discussion between worker and line manager is often the best way to proceed. Indeed, many problems and concerns are raised and settled in the course of everyday relationships and very few such concerns are going to turn into formal grievances.
- If the matter needs a more formal approach, follow the procedure.
- All organisations must provide employees with details of how to go about seeking redress of any work-related grievance, apart from those governed separately under the Health and Safety at Work Act 1974, and these grievance procedures should be agreed with representatives of any trade unions concerned. The procedures should be formal and should be given to employees in writing as part of their terms and conditions of service. Since 1993, employers have also been required to ensure that employees' written terms and conditions of employment include the name of 'a person to whom the employee can apply for the purposes of seeking redress of any grievance relating to employment and the manner in which any application should be made'. Under the Employment Relations Act 1999, the obligation to allow a worker to be accompanied has become a statutory right.
- Ensure everyone who might deal with a grievance is trained and understands the procedure.

- Set down simple procedures in writing which provide for prompt and confidential handling of grievances.
- Separate procedures might be necessary for sensitive areas such as discrimination, bullying and harassment and 'whistle-blowing'. A nominated contact within the organisation may be appropriate for fair treatment issues.
- If there is a grievance applying to more than one person, consider whether it should be resolved with any recognised trade union(s).
- The worker should put grievances raised under the formal procedure in writing.
- Hold a hearing in private. Make sure the worker is informed of his or her right to be accompanied.
- Have as open a discussion as possible about how the grievance might be resolved.
- Be calm and fair and do not make snap decisions.
- Ensure the hearing does not turn into any kind of disciplinary procedure.
- Seek external help if necessary, possibly in the form of a mediator.
- Inform the worker when he or she can expect a response.
- Respond to the worker's grievance in writing within the time limits specified in the procedure, and tell the worker of any further stages under the procedure.
- Provide for an appeal mechanism against any decision.
- Keep records, ensuring security and confidentiality and that they conform to the requirements of the Data Protection Act 1998.

Complementary to the handbook there is also a much shorter document – Code of Practice 1 Disciplinary and Grievance Procedures (2009), which employment tribunals will take into account when considering relevant cases, and will be able to adjust any awards made by up to 25 per cent for unreasonable failure to comply with the code. Essentially, this deals with issues of procedural and substantive fairness.

Applying these ideas to your own experience

What grievance procedures are laid down in your organisation? Are all your staff familiar with them?

A typical grievance procedure might have three stages in which, initially, an employee can verbally report dissatisfaction with any aspect of his or her employment to an immediate supervisor who will respond within an agreed timescale (this should be as short as possible). The supervisor is then responsible for investigating the grievance and, if possible, resolving it. If this is not possible or the employee remains dissatisfied with the outcome, he or she can state the grievance, usually in writing, to a line manager or departmental manager who will respond within an agreed timescale. If the matter remains unresolved, the line manager has to take it higher up and arrange for the employee to meet with someone more senior. If all else fails, and it is always preferable that problems are resolved internally, it may be necessary to bring in an independent third party to resolve the grievance.

When one of your staff comes to you with a complaint, however trivial, you need to establish all the facts as that person reports them and check these out with other people concerned. If you try to handle problems on the basis of inadequate or incorrect information, it is quite possible for you to contribute unwittingly to making them more serious. In most cases, unless you feel you are sure of all the facts surrounding a grievance, you should avoid making any comment immediately apart from promising to investigate the complaint fully – and following this up with prompt action. Ignoring a grievance can also cause it to grow. Your aim as a manager is to investigate the underlying cause of the grievance rather than to solve the immediate problem as the individual perceives it.

According to Bouwen and Salipante (1990), there are four distinct stages through which a grievance can pass, although the time taken at each stage will vary in individual cases. The first of these is the individual's perception of dissatisfaction or private formulation of a grievance. The person feels unfairly treated or perceives an action taken by someone else as being unfair. At this stage, the individual keeps his or her dissatisfaction private. When he or she decides to talk to other people about it – public formulation – there is a transformation of the grievance and it is likely to become distorted. At this stage, the person is looking for help and support, so he or she expresses the grievance in terms that are likely to elicit this kind of response. Instead of saying 'I don't get any recognition for all this extra work I'm doing', the person may state the grievance as 'None of us gets any recognition for all this extra work' in order to get the sympathy and support of colleagues and to make his or her own case stronger.

After public formulation of the grievance comes the stage of action which may involve a formal or informal statement of grievance to people with authority over the situation or such actions as working to rule, decreasing productivity or the level of service, calling in trade union support and so on. Finally, there will be an outcome; the grievance may be settled or it may result in some form of loss to the individual or the organisation through the ruling of an employment tribunal. The following box illustrates the type of issue that may occur.

A female personnel director claimed equal pay with the male merchandising director because their work was of equal value. She tried to resolve the matter through internal grievance procedures but was turned down. After informing the company chairman that she had submitted her claim to an employment tribunal, she went on holiday. She was dismissed on her return. The employment tribunal awarded her a six-figure sum in settlement of her claim on the grounds of equal pay, sex discrimination, unfair dismissal and breach of contract.

One method of reducing the potential severity of a grievance, which is becoming increasingly popular and appears to be very effective, is the creation of 'peer review committees' from among employees of the organisation. The person with the grievance and his or her supervisor can select a small panel from among a pool of the employee's peers who will be responsible for listening to the grievance and suggesting ways in which it might be resolved. There is a perceived fairness in this system since most people are more prepared to accept the judgement of a selection of their peers than that of a superior or even of an external agency. It can also speed up the process whereby the grievance is given a fair hearing and this can often reduce frustration created by the feeling that no one is taking any notice. The case in the box below illustrates this sort of issue.

In a case which went to an employment tribunal, a company changed the basis on which two salesmen were rewarded, resulting in a drop in pay. The salesmen attempted to have their grievances heard by the managing director and the chairman of the company, but were unsuccessful. They eventually resigned and claimed 'constructive dismissal' – which is so termed because it arises when an employee believes the employer leaves him/her no alternative but to terminate the employment contract. The employment tribunal decided that failure to use a grievance procedure amounted to breach of contract and the salesmen were able to claim damages from the company.

This case illustrates an important feature of grievance handling, that procedural considerations can be as important as substantive ones in deciding legal issues.

Managing discipline

Whereas grievances are initiated by the workers, discipline is initiated by the management. Again, and possibly even more so than in the case of grievances, it is necessary for a manager to tread very warily. Initiating disciplinary action should not be taken lightly. Employees, as you have seen, have the right to express their dissatisfaction about shortcomings and problems related to their jobs and working environments and should be encouraged to follow laid down grievance procedures. Disciplinary action should not be considered the result of, or even connected with, any genuine grievance voiced by an employee. As with grievance procedures, however, there is a legal obligation to provide employees with written details of disciplinary procedures within the organisation.

The Acas Advisory Handbook *Discipline and Grievances at Work* notes that it is important to look at ways of preventing disciplinary problems in the first place by following good policies in areas such as selection, induction, training, motivation and communication; by setting appropriate standards and rules in key areas such as absence, timekeeping, conduct and performance; and also the desirability of informal action by dealing with any issues as early as possible in order to 'nip in the bud' the need to take disciplinary action. The handbook suggests several reasons for having disciplinary rules, namely because:

- clear rules are necessary for promoting fairness and order in the treatment of individuals and in the conduct of employment relations
- they assist an organisation to operate effectively
- they set standards of conduct at work
- they provide a mechanism dealing with alleged failures to observe the rules
- they ensure that employees know what standards are expected of them
- they become important in evaluating the fairness of disciplinary decisions
- they are a legal requirement.

The Code of Practice 1 (2009), which is incorporated in the handbook and does have a legal status, suggests the following features of good disciplinary procedures. They should:

- be in writing
- specify to whom they apply
- be non-discriminatory
- provide for matters to be dealt with without undue delay
- provide for proceedings, witness statements and records to be kept confidential
- indicate the disciplinary actions which may be taken
- specify the levels of management which have the authority to take the various forms of disciplinary action
- provide for workers to be informed of the complaints against them and where possible all relevant evidence before any hearing
- provide workers with an opportunity to prepare and state their case and call any relevant witnesses before decisions are reached
- provide workers with the right to be accompanied
- ensure that – except in cases of gross misconduct – no employees are dismissed for a first breach of discipline
- ensure that disciplinary action is not taken until the case has been carefully investigated
- ensure that workers are given an explanation for any penalty imposed
- provide a right of appeal – normally to a more senior manager – and specify the procedure to be followed.

Although the handbook cannot be enforced legally, failure by employers to conform to the spirit of its contents will be noted in any subsequent action such as a claim for unfair dismissal.

A common disciplinary procedure used for all but cases of summary dismissal would include three stages. The first of these would be a verbal warning or, if the offence is more serious, a written warning, which sets out the nature of the offence and what is likely to happen if it continues or if there are further offences. If there is further misconduct, a final written warning is issued, which should contain a statement that any recurrence would lead to suspension or dismissal or some other penalty. If the misconduct still continues, the final stage might be a disciplinary transfer, suspension without pay or dismissal, depending on the offence.

Applying these ideas to your own experience

How do your staff find out about your organisation's disciplinary rules and regulations?

If there is a problem that involves violation of the rules, you need to know about it as quickly as possible. Check your facts – is the employee genuinely breaking a rule; does he or she realise this? If there does seem to be a real or potential problem, tell the employee about your concern and arrange to have a discussion about it.

At this stage, you are not invoking formal disciplinary procedures; you are trying to avoid that being necessary. In your discussion you need to find out if the employee realises he or she is breaking organisational rules and ask the employee what he or she is going to do about it. You should point out to the employee the potential penalties he or she might incur if formal disciplinary procedures are set in motion – not as a threat but as a statement of fact. The atmosphere of this meeting should be one of trust and support rather than of criticism. Your aim is to get the employee to understand what he or she is doing wrong and for you both to agree on a solution. If this method fails and you have to invoke the procedures, accept that this is necessary not only in order to improve the situation but to maintain your own authority and credibility with your staff.

In a case where a doctor had been dismissed by a National Health Service trust, the Supreme Court was prepared to grant an injunction because there were a number of procedural irregularities in the proceedings against Dr Chhabra which, especially when taken together, rendered the convening of the disciplinary panel a material breach of her contract of employment:

- having a biased person involved
- the trust's categorisation of Dr Chhabra's conduct as gross misconduct when it so clearly was not was itself sufficient grounds for an injunction
- the trust had relied on an example of gross misconduct in its policy ('serious breaches of information governance with regard to data protection, confidentiality and information security') which had only been included in the policy *after* the incidents in this case had taken place. In other words, it had not spelt out to its employees before that point that such conduct was so serious in its eyes.

(Acas Newsletter, April 2014)

Dismissal

Dismissal should be a last resort and employees have a right not to be unfairly dismissed. Since dismissal can have legal consequences, these are considered in the following chapter. However, even without the potential legal dimension, dismissal is a difficult and emotional task for managers, never mind the person who is being dismissed. Some simple guidelines may make it less stressful all round:

- provide for matters to be dealt with without undue delay
- provide for proceedings, witness statements and records to be kept confidential
- indicate the disciplinary actions which may be taken
- write a script to follow
- create a one-to-one situation free from disruptions
- set the scene then give the news clearly
- explain the decision but do not take too long in justifying it, and avoid recriminations
- the terms of the dismissal should be written and the employee should be given a copy
- try to suggest a positive future for the employee
- close the meeting decisively and do not allow it to drag on
- make notes on what took place and what was said.

Hopefully front-line managers will not have to dismiss someone very often.

Activities

1. Of the various challenging situations examined in this chapter, how many have you personally experienced? Do you think you handled them adequately? What more could you have done?
2. Obtain a copy of the Acas handbook *Discipline and Grievances at Work* (which is also available at www.Acas.org.uk). How far does your organisation live up to the content of the handbook in the way in which its procedures are laid out? Is there anything that you think ought to be changed?

References

Acas, (2009) Code of Practice 1 Disciplinary and Grievance Procedures. London.
Acas, (2014a) *Bullying and Harassment at Work: Guidance for Employees*. Available on-line at www.acas.org.uk/index.aspx?articleid=797 [accessed 14 January 2014].
Acas, (2014b) *Discipline and Grievances at Work – the Acas Guide*. London.
Acas, (2014 March and April) *Newsletters*. London.
Bouwen R. and Salipante P. F., (1990) 'Behavioural analysis of grievances: episodes, actions, and outcomes', *Employee Relations*, 12(4), 27–32.

easyJet, (2013) 'Employee rights and working conditions'. Available on-line at http:// corporate.easyjet.com/corporate-responsibility/business-principles/employee-rights-working-conditions.aspx?sc_lang=en.

International Labour Organization, (1965) International Labour Conference Report, 7(1): Examination of Grievances and Communication within the Undertaking. Geneva, ILO.

Janes H., (2013) 'Stress costs the economy', 18 March. Available on-line at www.stress-busting.co.uk.

People Management (October 2013), 26.

Thomas K. W., (2002) *Introduction to Conflict Management*. Mountain View, California, CPP.

Tovey A., (2013) 'Bank boss's break shows stress needs to be taken seriously', *The Telegraph*, 15 October. Available on-line from www.telegraph.co.uk/finance/jobs/10381393/Bank-bosss-break-shows-stress-needs-to-be-taken-seriously.html [accessed 15 January 2014].

Warr P. B., (1987) *Work, Unemployment and Mental Health*. Oxford, Oxford University Press.

9 The regulation of behaviour at work

Introduction

In this chapter we deal with the implications for managing people of the legal system and the institutions that complement it. Over the last 50 years employment law has become one of the most complex and regularly modified parts of the legal system, and also one of the most politically contentious, because law is an important source of power in the employment relationship. Managers not infrequently have to face situations which could have legal consequences; most of course do not result in any drastic development, which is just as well if work is to have continuity and stability, but managers need to be aware of what might be involved in a given situation. It cannot be overstated that the best way of avoiding any problem is for managers themselves to be aware of the principles of the law, if not the details. At the organisational level there are likely to be rules that will have legal consequences and managers need to be aware of the implications of these.

Many larger organisations employ specialist staff to deal with personnel-related matters and it is their responsibility to keep up to date with the many and frequent changes in the law. This is quite a daunting task even for experts. However, even in organisations with this facility, the front-line manager is likely to be the initial person involved in any formal grievance or disciplinary matters. On a day-to-day basis, you may have to deal with the first signs of trouble and, if there is no handy personnel department, with subsequent action. In many cases, it is the front-line manager's responsibility to deal with cases of grievance or to become involved in disciplinary action when this becomes inevitable; it is also his or her responsibility to offer help and advice to staff who have work-related problems and, where necessary, to recommend that they seek professional advice, possibly from the Advisory, Conciliation and Arbitration Service (Acas).

This chapter will cover the following issues:

- the legal and institutional framework of employment
- the principles of the employment relationship
- pay
- discrimination
- job security
- health and safety at work

- unfair dismissal
- redundancy
- parental rights
- transfers of undertakings
- working time
- whistle-blowing
- the legal framework of collective bargaining
- wider rights in the employment context.

The legal and institutional framework of employment

Patterns of relations in employment have changed considerably in the last 30 years in Britain. There is now less collective conflict, which was initially replaced by increasing numbers of individuals going to employment tribunals, but this trend after about 2009 has been reversed, and with radical changes in 2013 the numbers of cases going to tribunals have dropped dramatically. The law has also changed very considerably, in part to reduce the power of unions, but also to fit in with the emerging scope and importance of European legal frameworks incorporated into British law, and now, more recently, as part of the Employment Law Review undertaken from the election of the Coalition Government in May 2010 as an ongoing activity to re-evaluate the systems, procedures, roles and regulations surrounding the key institutions, as well as some of the content of employment law.

Some of these modifications were incorporated in the Enterprise and Regulatory Reform Act 2013, which goes well beyond employment law. Moreover, change is likely to continue, and especially so if the relationship between Britain and Europe were to alter. Thus, what is provided here is not necessarily, when you read it, the most up-to-date situation in what is already a very complex field.

The most important of the institutions in British employment relations are Acas, the employment (previously industrial) tribunals and the Equality and Human Rights Commission, which will now be briefly examined.

The Advisory, Conciliation and Arbitration Service (Acas)

Acas was created in 1975 and covers the three areas its title suggests. It has come to be a trusted third-party agency, which must take some of the credit for the improvement in British industrial and employment relations. Its advisory work is perhaps the least publicised but most important part of its work and involves providing information and advice and promoting good practice. We have already mentioned the Acas Handbook and Code of Practice for Discipline and Grievances at Work, and there are numerous others which provide valuable guidance to best practice in the workplace, based on the experiences of its staff and backed by the Acas Council, which represents both sides of industry. These publications are regularly updated and new issues covered. These guidance publications had over 750,000 downloads during 2013–14, and there were 4.6 million visits to the Acas website and an e-newsletter to 149,000 subscribers for those wishing to have ongoing updates on new developments.

Beyond its publications Acas provides both general and specific advice. In 2012–13 it operated 666 key points briefings, offered in-company training in 949 organisations with 18,137 delegates, ran open access programmes for 9,178 delegates, specific programmes for small companies (SMEs) which attracted 4,456 delegates, 250 in-depth business support projects, 2,324 telephone advice sessions involving complex issues and 1,340 face-to-face advisory meetings also on complex issues. In addition, Acas received 930,000 enquiries for information or advice at its system of public enquiry points located in its regional offices, of which 56 per cent came from individual employees and 35 per cent were concerned with discipline, dismissal or grievance issues. Most of these could be dealt with on the phone, but some required letters or occasionally personal interviews. Many of these enquiries came from people, either employers or employees, in small business, who were unclear about aspects of the increasingly complex legal requirements. Although there has been a decline in the more formal aspects of Acas' work such as conciliation, mediation and arbitration, most of these advisory aspects have continued to increase.

The second area in which Acas has a statutory duty is to promote settlement of a wide range of employment rights complaints which have been or could be made to an employment tribunal. This is called individual conciliation, and much of this work is handled on the phone by Acas staff. Table 9.1 illustrates the topics or

Table 9.1 Breakdown of cases going to conciliation in 2011–12, 2012–13 and 2013–14

Jurisdiction	2013–14	2012–13	2011–12
Unfair dismissal	24,306	37,598	40,580
Breach of contract	14,144	23,849	25,475
Wages Act	13,741	24,269	24,854
Working time	11,632	19,807	19,998
Disability discrimination	5,098	6,976	7,302
Redundancy pay	4,958	9,193	10,388
Sex discrimination	3,636	5,213	5,801
Race discrimination	2,846	4,288	4,579
Public interest disclosure	2,032	2,338	2,193
Provision of terms and conditions	1,820	2,917	1,049
Age discrimination	1,473	2,235	2,796
Maternity detriment	1,207	1,494	1,688
Religious discrimination	541	846	858
Sexual orientation discrimination	347	591	588
Other	6,226	10,401	9,467
Total jurisdictions	94,007	155,015	159,151
Total cases	40,938	67,827	72,075

Source: Acas Annual Report 2013–14, p. 29
© Crown copyright (2001–2009)

Table 9.2 Disposal of conciliation cases in 2011–12, 2012–13 and 2013–14

Outcomes	2013–14	2012–13	2011–12
Struck out	4,073	4,254	4,883
Settled	23,519	29,973	32,120
Withdrawn	13,052	15,417	17,659
Default judgement	2,445	3,741	3,921
Heard by tribunal	14,930	13,677	15,366
Total	59,019	67,062	73,949

Source: Acas Annual Report 2013–14, p. 30

jurisdictions that cases covered, and it should be noted that many cases cover more than one jurisdiction, whilst table 9.2 indicates the way in which cases were disposed of, with the largest group being settled at conciliation and only some 20 per cent being heard at the tribunal stage in 2012–13 and 24 per cent in 2013–14. This latter year incorporated the introduction of fees (of which more later) when applying to a tribunal and, as the figures show, this has had a dramatic impact on the number of cases.

The third aspect of Acas' responsibilities is that of collective dispute conciliation and resolution. The number of requests for collective conciliation was 858 in 2013–14 as compared to 875 in 2012–13 (and 1,910 in 1980), and the rate of successful conclusion was over 90 per cent, a tribute to Acas' impartiality and its experience over the last 40 years. Almost half the cases dealt with pay and/or other terms and conditions, with the next most important being trade union recognition, other trade union matters, changes in working practices, discipline/dismissal, and redundancy. The final stage of this side of Acas' activity is arbitration or dispute mediation, and in 2013–14 there were 15 cases, as compared with 17 in 2012–13. This is a much smaller number than in the first few years of the life of Acas (322 in 1980). Arbitration is a situation where the parties must agree to accept the decision of the independent arbitrator drawn from the Acas panel of experts, although this is not strictly legally binding, and dispute mediation is where the parties are provided with a recommended solution. In addition, there were also 119 joint problem-solving activities.

Employment tribunals and courts

Employment tribunals were first created as industrial tribunals in 1964, but their name was changed to employment tribunals by the Employment Rights Act of 1998. Normally, the tribunals consist of a legally qualified chairperson and two lay members, reflecting on the one hand nominations by employer organisations and on the other employee organisations. However, the lay members are not expected to represent the interests of their nominating organisations, but rather to use their judgement independently. The average cost to an employer of defending a case is about £8,500, which can be compared with an average out of court settlement of £4,500. To give another perspective, between May 2010 and April 2014, the UK Parliament spent over £100,000 fighting 16 claims at employment tribunals.

Hearings are expected to be relatively informal, but there has been concern at increasing legalism and bureaucracy. An employment tribunal is required to follow the decisions of higher courts, which comprise the Employment Appeal Tribunal (EAT), the Court of Appeal and the House of Lords. In turn, all British courts must follow the guidance given by the European Court of Justice (ECJ); when a British court or tribunal decides that clarification of European law is necessary for it to make a decision, it will remit the matter to the ECJ. The European Union can create various types of legislation, the most important being regulations and directives. Regulations are generally of a broad nature and are directly applicable to all Member States. Directives are instruments that require Member States to translate the contents of the directive into national law and they are given two or three years to implement this. National courts also have an obligation to interpret national law in such a way that it gives effect to EU law.

From July 2013 employees have been required to lodge a fee to submit a claim, with another fee if the claim is heard by a tribunal, although in some cases where employees are on low pay, the fees may be waived. Basically, the fees to submit a claim are £160 for type A, which are for straightforward issues, or £250 for more complicated issues such as dismissal, discrimination or whistle-blowing under the Public Information Disclosure Act, whilst the fee to hear the claim may be up to £950. If the claim is successful, the employee may apply to have the fee covered by the employer. Moreover, as of April 2014, there was a significant change in the procedures for making a claim to a tribunal. An employee considering a claim against his employer must now inform Acas of this intent, and Acas will engage in a process called early conciliation, which is free, impartial, non-judgemental and confidential in attempting to resolve the differences between the parties. If the matter is not resolved Acas will issue a certificate, which is now required to submit a claim to a tribunal. These two changes have already had a major impact on the number of cases coming forward, as can be seen in table 9.1.

The Equality and Human Rights Commission and the Equality Act 2010

The Commission (EHRC) has responsibility for the promotion and enforcement of equality and non-discrimination laws in England, Scotland and Wales. In 2006 it took over the responsibilities of three former commissions: the Commission for Racial Equality, the Equal Opportunities Commission and the Disability Rights Commission. It also has responsibility for other aspects of equality: age, sexual orientation and religion or belief. Its role is to ensure that:

(a) people's ability to achieve their potential is not limited by prejudice or discrimination
(b) there is respect for and protection of each individual's human rights (including respect for the dignity and worth of each individual)

(c)   each person has an equal opportunity to participate in society
(d)   there is mutual respect between communities based on understanding and valuing of diversity and on shared respect for equality and human rights.

Many of the issues relating to these activities come within the world of work and are therefore part of employment relations.

The EHRC needs to be seen in conjunction with the Equality Act of 2010, which brings together over 116 separate pieces of legislation into one single Act. The Act harmonises the current legislation to provide Britain with a new discrimination law, which protects individuals from unfair treatment and promotes a fair and more equal society.

The nine main pieces of legislation that have merged are:

- the Equal Pay Act 1970
- the Sex Discrimination Act 1975
- the Race Relations Act 1976
- the Disability Discrimination Act 1995
- the Employment Equality (Religion or Belief) Regulations 2003
- the Employment Equality (Sexual Orientation) Regulations 2003
- the Employment Equality (Age) Regulations 2006
- the Equality Act 2006, Part 2
- the Equality Act (Sexual Orientation) Regulations 2007.

You will read more about these areas during the chapter.

The principles of the employment relationship

We now move to the scope of law and legislation. There is an element of common law in the concept of the contract of employment, which can be entered into informally even though a considerable degree of formality is desirable because of the consequences of having an employee. It is in fact very important that all the relevant terms and conditions are clearly understood at the time employment commences; nevertheless, many of the practical and legal difficulties and lack of clarity which give rise to so many enquiries to Acas are due to these issues not being sorted out at the point of employment. This is in spite of the fact that there is a legal obligation to provide a statement of particulars no later than two months after the start of employment, and these include: the identity of the parties; the date of employment; the rate of payment and the intervals at which it will be paid; any conditions relating to hours of work; holidays and holiday pay; incapacity to work through sickness or injury; the length of notice; the job title or brief description of the work to be done; any collective agreements affecting the employment; and grievance and disciplinary rules and procedures. The statement of particulars is not the whole of the contract of employment, however, and some of it may be informal and based on custom and practice. Terms may also be derived from collective agreements, works rules and statute law, as well as those aspects individually determined. Changes cannot be made to a contract of employment without the consent of the employee, but the employee may be deemed to have agreed to the change if he or she does not explicitly reject it.

The existence of a contract of employment imposes certain obligations on both the employer and the employee, the breaking of which constitutes a breach of the contract of employment. These are based on both long-established common law principles and more recent statutory developments. The main duties of the employer are:

*   to pay wages
*   to provide work, although employees who receive their full contractual remuneration cannot normally complain if they are idle
*   to cooperate with the employee. This has been interpreted to mean that the employer must not upset the mutual trust on which cooperation is based, although each case must be determined on the facts
*   to take reasonable care of the employee. This is both a general duty and one which involves various statutes in the health and safety area
*   to provide references, although strictly speaking this refers to ex-employees.

Employees also have duties, as listed below:

*   to cooperate with the employer, especially the duty to obey lawful and reasonable orders and not to impede the employer's business
*   to be loyal, such that the employee's own interests should not conflict with the duty he or she owes to the employer; in particular the duty not to compete with the employer and the duty not to disclose confidential information
*   to take reasonable care. If employees do not, there is an implied duty to indemnify the employer against the consequences of their negligence.

In a case reported in 2002, *Lister* v. *Hedley Hall* ([2001] UKHL 22), the House of Lords revolutionised the concept of vicarious liability by focusing on the closeness of the connection between the employee's job and the wrongdoing. On this basis the employers of a school warden could be liable for his sexual assaults on schoolchildren because he was employed to look after them. It did not matter that what he had done was outside what he was authorised by his employers to do.

We now move to the more specific areas of employment law.

Pay

Pay is normally settled by express terms of the contract of employment, but the Equal Pay Act 1970 (now part of the Equality Act 2010) established obligations for equality of pay and the National Minimum Wage Act of 1998 established a minimum wage; this is reset annually after guidance from the Low Pay Commission and in October 2014 it was set at £6.50 for over 21-year-olds, £5.13 for

18–20-year-olds, £3.79 for under 18-year-olds finished with compulsory education and £2.73 for under 19-year-olds or first year apprentices.

Employers must give their employees itemised pay statements. Deductions from wages are unlawful unless approved by statute or by agreement with the employee. Employers are also responsible for paying statutory sick pay for up to 28 weeks of absence in a single period of entitlement. A right to sick pay may be inferred in the contract of employment by custom and practice or the knowledge of the parties when the contract was originated. Notification of absence must be given to the employer in accordance with rules laid down for employees.

Finally, employers are obliged to keep records showing the amount paid to each employee.

Discrimination

Issues relating to discrimination have become more significant as the extent of diversity in the labour force has increased, something which was noted in Chapter 4, and this area is now one of the most complex, even if its intentions are simple. The Equality Act 2010 identifies a range of characteristics under which discrimination is unlawful, including race, religion, disability, age and sex (including sexual orientation and gender reassignment). Maternity also creates certain obligations. Employers have a legal responsibility to take such steps as are reasonably practicable to prevent unlawful discrimination.

There are four types of discrimination:

- direct, in which a person is treated unfavourably because of the characteristic
- indirect, where a policy disadvantages someone with a particular characteristic
- harassment, when unwanted conduct related to the characteristic has the effect of violating a person's dignity, or creating an intimidating, hostile, degrading, humiliating or offensive environment
- victimisation, namely unfair treatment of a person who has made or supported a complaint about discrimination.

UK and EU law divide discrimination into direct and indirect forms. Direct discrimination means treating a person of a protected characteristic less favourably than a comparable person who does not share that characteristic. This is an objective test, so that it is irrelevant what motive the employer had. Even if it was 'positive' discrimination, in the sense that the purpose was to help an underprivileged group, this is still unlawful.

Originally a sub-category of direct discrimination, harassment is now an independent tort, which requires no comparator. The Protection from Harassment Act 1997, and now the Equality Act 2010, define harassment as where a person's dignity is violated, or the person is subject to an intimidating, hostile, degrading, humiliating or offensive environment. An employer will be liable for its own conduct, but also conduct of employees, or customers if this happens on two or more occasions and the employer could be reasonably expected to have intervened.

It is hard for anyone to complain about harassment because of the embarrassment, and often harder for men to complain than women, because of their social conditioning.

In *Ladele* v. *Islington LBC* ([2009] EWCA Civ 1357), a woman who refused to register gay civil partners because she said her Christianity made her conclude homosexuality was wrong was dismissed for not carrying out her duties, and in *Eweida* v. *British Airways plc* ([2010] EWCA Civ 80), a woman who wished to wear a cross claimed that BA's instruction to remove it was indirectly discriminatory against Christians. Both claims failed because it was held that neither antipathy towards homosexuals nor crucifix jewellery are essential parts of the Christian religion.

Because treating disabled people equally based on ability to perform tasks could easily result in the persistence of exclusion from the workforce, employers are bound to do as much as reasonably possible to ensure participation is not hindered in practice. Under the Equality Act 2010, employers have to make 'reasonable adjustments', for example in changing a workplace practice if it would create a disadvantage, changing physical features of a workplace or providing auxiliary aids to work.

Outside the Equality Act, and the EU directives that target discrimination based on a fixed status, the law has a series of measures, albeit weaker, to counteract discrimination against people who hold non-permanent contracts. An important reason for the trio of the Part-time Workers Directive, the Fixed-term Work Directive and the Temporary and Agency Work Directive is that people doing such work often fall into the same groups as those seeking protection under the Equality Act. Each is implemented by domestic legislation, but all have come under criticism for their restrictive nature. The Part-time Workers (Prevention of Less Favourable Treatment) Regulations 2000 state that part-time workers cannot, without objective justification, be treated less favourably than a comparable full-time worker.

The Agency Workers Regulations 2010 provide protection against less favourable treatment when workers arrive at work through an employment agency. Here the regulation is again more limited, as agency workers are explicitly entitled merely to equal treatment in 'basic working conditions', which is defined as their pay and their working time.

Indirect discrimination occurs when an employer applies a requirement or condition that would apply equally to all groups but which is such that the proportion of people from a particular grouping who can comply with it is considerably smaller than that of persons from another grouping.

In recruitment and selection, it is unlawful to discriminate in the arrangements made for recruitment, in the terms offered, or by refusing to offer employment. A wide range of practices could be problematic, from the wording of advertisements to word of mouth only recruitment or refusing to employ those who live in a particular geographical area.

Nevertheless, discrimination can be lawful in certain circumstances, such as where sex or race is an occupational requirement or where discrimination is necessary in order to comply with a statute, such as in the health and safety area.

Within employment, discrimination is not permitted in respect of any opportunities for training or promotion, or any benefits or facilities. As might be expected, discrimination is also not permitted in the area of dismissal, for whatever reason.

A black head chef was awarded £20,634 after an industrial tribunal found that he had been sacked because of his race. The chef, who was of Nigerian origin, was dismissed following a takeover of the restaurant where he worked in Chelsea. The chef, who had an unblemished record, received no warning of his dismissal and the company who had taken over the restaurant refused to supply him with a reference (Acas Newsletter, April 2014).

Both employers and individuals may be sued. Individuals are liable for performing or putting pressure on someone to perform an unlawful act. Employers are not only liable directly, but also for the actions of their employees, even if the actions were done without the employer's knowledge or approval, unless the employer had taken all reasonably practical steps to prevent them.

Denise alleged that the store manager had made sexual gestures to her when they were alone. Another female employee made similar complaints. They complained to more senior management but no investigation occurred until, on union advice, written complaints were sent to their regional manager. Eventually all were interviewed. The manager remained at work during this time. He was told to apologise and Denise was offered a transfer. This was sex discrimination since there was a case of clear harassment, there had been a very slow response during which time the victim was left at work and she, not the harasser, was expected to move. The employer was liable as the manager was exercising his supervisory duties when he harassed Denise. An employment tribunal awarded compensation of £3,500 to Denise for injured feelings.

Since it is unusual to find evidence of direct discrimination, a case will usually depend on what inferences it is proper to draw from the facts uncovered at the tribunal.

Under the equal pay aspects of the Equality Act 2010, an equality clause operates when a person is employed on 'like work' to a person of the opposite sex in the same employment. The concept of like work is focused on the job, rather than the person performing it. It is for the employer to show that any differences in pay are due to a genuine material difference not related to the sex of either employee.

In a case concerning equal pay brought against North Yorkshire County Council, the Law Lords ruled that women should receive the same rate as men. The Council had argued that it needed to compete with private contractors in a competitive tendering process and the only way it could do this effectively was to pay the women at lower rates. The Law Lords' decision was particularly important in a prevailing climate where services are increasingly being contracted-out and pressures to reduce costs remain intense.

The disability part of the Equality Act 2010 makes it unlawful for all but very small employers to discriminate against existing or potential employees for reasons relating to their disability. A disability is defined as an impairment which has a substantial and long-term adverse effect on an ability to carry out normal day-to-day activities.

Faith schools in England and Wales are granted exemptions from equality legislation, allowing them to apply a religious test in appointing, remunerating and promoting teachers. Teachers in such schools can be disciplined or dismissed for conduct which is 'incompatible with the precepts of the school's religion'. Kath Brown, chair of governors at Corpus Christi, is reported at Wales Online as saying: 'due to the marital position of Mr (Christopher) Belli' the school had decided 'that it is not appropriate for him to assume the headteacher post'. An acting head and deputy head were put in place for the next academic year, starting in September. Anne Robertson, schools director for the Archdiocese of Cardiff, said developments at Corpus Christi were 'relatively unusual' – but not unprecedented (Acas Newsletter April 2014).

Job security

UK workers have three principal job security rights, now consolidated in the Employment Rights Act 1996. These statutory provisions override the old common law position that a dismissal would only be wrongful if it contravened the contract's express or implied terms. First, after one month's work an employee must have one week's notice before dismissal. Second, after one year's work, the dismissal must be for a good business reason. If an employment tribunal is not convinced the dismissal is justified on grounds of an employee's capability, conduct, redundancy or another good reason, the dismissal will be unfair and the employee will be awarded damages. A court may order that an employee should get his or her job back, but this is rare. Third, after two years' work and if dismissed, an employee is entitled to a redundancy payment, which like the notice period increases according to the number of years worked. Contracts typically go beyond this bare minimum, but cannot go below.

Health and safety at work

One of the main terms that accompany the employment relationship is that the employer will provide a safe system of work, and the common law remains relevant for obtaining civil law compensation. In principle, the employer is vicariously liable for all actions of people acting for them in the course of employment, and under the Employers' Liability (Compulsory Insurance) Act 1969 employers must take out insurance for all injury costs. The main statute in this area is the Health and Safety at Work Act 1974, whilst the Management of Health and Safety at Work Regulations 1992 make more explicit what the employer is required to do to manage health and safety under the Act. Both apply to every work activity, and furthermore seek to protect those outside the work context from health and safety risks arising out of work.

The Health and Safety Executive provides guidance, codes of practice and regulations for specific working contexts, and these are kept in line with European-wide harmonised directives. Enforcement can also be delegated to local authorities. However, the Enterprise and Regulatory Reform Act 2013 limits the right to claim for compensation to where it can be proved that an employer acted negligently, so that the employer will have the defence of having taken reasonable steps to reduce the risk of an accident.

Every employer with five or more employees must prepare a written statement of policy on health and safety at work and the arrangements for carrying out that policy. Employers must also distribute leaflets or display posters about the requirements of health and safety law. They must also conduct a risk assessment to identify what needs to be done to comply with legal requirements. Certain accidents, incidents or injuries must be reported if they occur in connection with work. Unfortunately, accidents at work are still an all too common occurrence; between 2001 and 2014, 448 British soldiers were killed in Afghanistan, whilst over the same period, more than 760 construction workers were killed on British sites.

Employers must also consult employees and their representatives, who may be trade union appointed or directly elected. The representatives can call for the setting up of a safety committee at the place of work, and it is recommended that they should be given time off with pay to undertake training in the safety area. As an employer, it is necessary to provide:

* a safe place of work
* a safe means of access to the place of work
* a safe system of work
* adequate materials
* competent fellow employees
* protection from unnecessary risk of injury
* a safety policy
* adequate instruction and training
* a safety committee if union-appointed safety representatives ask for one.

Unfair dismissal

Wrongful dismissal refers to a termination of employment which contravenes a contract's terms, whether expressly agreed or implied by the courts. In contrast to wrongful dismissal, which is an action for unjustified breach of the terms of an employment contract, unfair dismissal is a claim based in the Employment Rights Act 1996, which governs the reasons for when a contract is terminated. Under the Act, any employee who is employed for over one year (or two for those whose employment started after 21 March 2011) may claim for an employment tribunal (composed of a judge, an employer and an employee representative) to review the decision of the employee's dismissal, and to obtain a remedy if the dismissal was not fair within the meaning of the Act.

The legislation is complex and an employer needs to be very sure that it has good reasons for fair dismissal before embarking on the process. Any employee has the right to be given a chance to improve his or her work performance or conduct, to be given a chance to explain the reasons for his or her behaviour and to exercise the right to appeal against dismissal. Proper notice, according to the employee's contract, must be given, orally and in writing.

There are various qualifications and exclusions to the right not to be unfairly dismissed, in particular the need to have one year's (two years for those whose employment started after 21 March 2011) continuous service and to be under normal retirement age.

An employee is treated as dismissed if the contract of employment is terminated by the employer with or without notice, a fixed-term contract comes to an end or the employee terminates the contract as a result of the employer's conduct. This latter is known as constructive dismissal, and requires that the employer has breached the central tenets of the contract of employment.

A modification of the ending of the contract of employment was inaugurated by a Statutory Code of Practice under the Enterprise and Regulatory Reform Act 2013 through the creation of settlement agreements. These are legally binding contracts that can be used to end the employment relationship on agreed terms. Their main feature is that they waive the individual's right to make a claim to a court or tribunal on matters that are specifically covered in the agreement. They usually include some form of payment by the employer and may also include a reference. Certain conditions apply, notably that the employee must have received advice from a 'relevant independent adviser'.

In making a complaint, the employee must show that he or she was dismissed. The effective date of termination of employment is the date on which notice expires or on which termination otherwise takes effect.

Once dismissal is accepted, the burden is on the employer to show the reason, or principal reason, for the dismissal and, for the dismissal to be fair, it must fall within one of five categories:

- The capacity or qualifications of the employee for performing work of the type for which the employee was employed.
- The conduct of the employee.
- The employee was redundant.
- The employee could not continue to work without a statutory contravention being involved.
- Some other substantial reason.

Each of these potentially fair reasons is a complex area of law in its own right as the reasons have been interpreted and created precedents.

There is also a range of circumstances in which dismissal will automatically be unfair, including the assertion of a statutory right, various family reasons including pregnancy, aspects of health and safety law, and trade union membership or non-membership.

The key decision to be made by the tribunal is about reasonableness in the circumstances. More specifically:

> the determination of the question whether the dismissal was fair or unfair
>
> (a) depends on whether in the circumstances (including the size and administrative resources of the employer's undertaking) the employer acted reasonably or unreasonably in treating it as a sufficient reason for dismissing the employee, and
>
> (b) shall be determined in accordance with equity and the substantial merits of the case.

Employers will be expected to treat employees in similar circumstances in a similar way. Nevertheless, each case will be decided on its own facts and with the capacity to consider both mitigating circumstances and aggravating factors. Employees cannot claim unfairness if they are dismissed while taking part in unofficial industrial action.

Procedural fairness is important as well as substantive fairness. Indeed, a key issue is not only why someone is dismissed, but how they are dismissed. The Acas Code of Practice 1 – Disciplinary and Grievance Procedures (2009), key parts of which were outlined in Chapter 8, is a substantial consideration here. Whilst it does not have the force of law, it will weigh heavily against an employer if it is not followed. Natural justice is an important feature of procedural fairness. An accused person should know the case against him or her and be able to dispute it and should be able to request that he or she is accompanied by a companion, whether a union official or a friend.

Tribunals have a number of possible findings in dismissal situations. They can find the dismissal to be fair, or they can find it to be unfair, in which case there are three main alternative remedies. These are reinstatement, re-engagement and compensation. The first two remedies are relatively rare, and are dependent on the dismissed employee wanting re-employment and the practicality of such an order.

Compensation usually consists of a basic award and a compensatory award. The basic award is calculated in the same way as a redundancy payment (see below), whilst a compensatory award is what the tribunal 'considers just and equitable in all the circumstances having regard to the loss sustained by the complainant in consequence of the dismissal insofar as that loss is attributable to action taken by the employer' (Employment Rights Act 1996). It is up to the complainant to prove the loss, which is defined under a number of headings. Some of these, such as loss of pension rights, can be very complex calculations.

The maximum amount of a compensatory award was raised considerably in the Employment Relations Act 1999 to £50,000 and is now increased according to the retail price index. The maximum compensatory award in 2014 was £74,200. Employees dismissed after 29 July 2013 are subject to a compensatory cap, which means their award is limited to 52 weeks' pay or £74,200, whichever is the lower. Tribunals can adjust awards up or down by up to 25 per cent if they think that either party unreasonably failed to follow the Acas Code of Practice.

Other important dimensions of calculating compensation for unfair dismissal and redundancy are continuity of employment, normal working hours and a week's pay, each of which has legal implications. Thus, normal working hours are those required by the contract of employment and do not include non-contractual overtime, whilst a week's pay is the gross amount payable for a week under the contract of employment.

As can be seen from Table 9.1, there has been a very considerable drop in the number of unfair dismissal cases coming before tribunals as a result of changes in the rules of access in 2013. Nevertheless, the impact of an unfair dismissal case can be very considerable. A Royal British Legion Club, which was ordered to pay a former employee £70,000 for unfair dismissal, has closed. The Legion building on Ashley Road in Boscombe has been put on the market more than three years after it was ordered to pay the compensation to a former bar steward (Acas newsletter, April 2014).

Redundancy

Redundancy is a major feature of the British labour market; in the four years from 2008 to 2012, 2.7 million people were made redundant, at a cost of £28.6 billion. Moreover, if a company goes into liquidation and cannot pay redundancy costs, the government must pick up the bill, which can be substantial; when Woolworths collapsed in 2008 the government had to pay costs of £67 million, and it faces another large payment as a result of a decision by a tribunal that Comet failed to consult staff properly before its failure in 2012.

Redundancy is a potentially fair reason for dismissal, but it carries a number of important dimensions of its own. It is defined as where the employer has or will have a diminution of the requirement of work of a particular kind. The burden of proof is on the employer to show that any offer of alternative employment was suitable and rejection by the employee was unreasonable. There may be a trial period to consider offers of alternative employment.

The employer should give as much warning as possible to enable the employees or the unions to consider possible alternatives or seek alternative work. There are specific consultation requirements where an employer is proposing to make redundant 20 or more employees in an establishment in a period of 90 days or less.

Calculating redundancy payments is based on the following formula: one and a half week's pay for each year of continuous employment in which the employee is aged between 41 and 64; one week's pay for each year in which the individual was aged between 22 and 40; and half a week's pay for each year between the ages of 18 and 21. There is a maximum of 20 years and a limit to the basic weekly pay that can be claimed, currently in 2014 £450 per week.

> British Aerospace made 500 workers redundant out of its workforce of 7,000. Workers were assessed against six criteria and marked on one of four grades. The points were added up and those with the lowest scores were made redundant. Of those involved, 234 complained of unfair selection for redundancy, mainly on grounds of lack of consultation and unfairness in the selection procedure.

Selection for redundancy can be a minefield of legal requirements. The main requirements for fair dismissal for redundancy are as follows:

*   The redundancy is genuine and is not being claimed by the employer as the reason for dismissing an incompetent employee.
*   The people selected for redundancy have been chosen on the basis of agreed criteria, which may be criteria agreed within the company or in agreement with the trade union.
*   Elected employee representatives or independent trade unions have been consulted.
*   There is no suitable alternative work available; the organisation is required to try to find alternative work for employees rather than declare them redundant.
*   Redundancy selection does not contravene the Equality Act 2010.

For small scale redundancies, Acas provides a step-by-step guide starting from considering alternatives and developing a plan, to briefing managers and talking to staff, in which there is a requirement to consult meaningfully. Then the steps move to choosing redundant staff carefully, giving redundancy notice and pay, remembering any notice period rights and allowing staff to appeal against their selection for redundancy. Finally, there should be a focus on the future of the business.

There are extra legal requirements when 20 or more staff are to be made redundant within a period of 90 days. When compulsory redundancies are unavoidable and the employer must select among a group of workers, the procedure the employer follows must be procedurally fair, or the workforce will have an unfair dismissal claim. In *Williams v. Compare Maxam Ltd* ([1982] ICR 156) it was held that, in response to managers who had selected workers to lose their jobs based on personal preference, the proper steps should be: (1) to give all warning possible; (2) to consult the union; (3) to agree objective criteria; (4) to follow those criteria; and (5) always to check if there is alternative employment rather than dismissal. An employee should accept a reasonable offer for redeployment, and will lose entitlement to redundancy if he or she declines it.

Parental rights

A pregnant woman is entitled to paid time off for antenatal care. It is automatically unfair to dismiss a woman by reason of her pregnancy. Maternity leave is divided into ordinary (up to 18 weeks), compulsory (not less than two weeks after childbirth, included in the ordinary leave period) and additional (up to 29 weeks after childbirth) leave periods. Statutory maternity pay is available for a maximum of eight weeks. A woman is entitled to return to her job under the original contract of employment and on terms and conditions not less favourable than would have occurred had she not been absent.

If an employee has completed one year's service with an employer, the employee is entitled to 18 weeks of unpaid parental leave for each child born or adopted. The leave can start once the child is born or placed for adoption, or as soon as the employee has completed a year's service, whichever is the later. Employees can take the leave at any time up to the child's fifth birthday (or until five years after placement in the case of adoption). If the child has disabilities, employees can take 18 weeks up to the child's 18th birthday.

A request should be made to an employer giving 21 days' notice of the start date of the parental leave; the employer may ask for this to be in writing. As long as the employee qualifies for parental leave and gives the employer the correct notice the employee should be able to take parental leave at any time.

To take parental leave straight after the birth or adoption of a child, an employee should give notice 21 days before the beginning of the expected week of childbirth or placement. In cases where this may not be possible, employees should give notice to the employer as soon as possible, for example, if a child is born prematurely or where less than 21 days' notice is given that a child is to be placed with you for adoption.

Parental leave should be taken in blocks of a week or multiples of a week, and should not be taken as 'odd' days off, unless the employer agrees otherwise or the child is disabled. Employees cannot take off more than four weeks during a year. A week is based on an employee's working pattern.

An employee will remain employed while on parental leave and some terms of the contract, such as contractual notice and redundancy terms, still apply.

Under a new system of flexible parental leave to be introduced in 2015, parents will be able to choose how they share care of their child in the first year after birth. Employed mothers will still be entitled to 52 weeks' maternity leave; however, working parents will be able to opt to share the leave.

Mothers will have to take at least the initial two weeks of leave following the birth as a recovery period. Following that they can choose to end the maternity leave and the parents can opt to share the remaining leave as flexible parental leave.

The right to request flexible working in a more general way has also been available for carers, but as from the end of June 2014 the government has extended the right to request flexible working to all employees and removing the pre-existing statutory procedure for considering requests. Instead, employers will have a duty to consider all requests in a reasonable manner; however, employers will continue to have the flexibility to refuse requests on business grounds.

Employees are also entitled to take reasonable time off for incidents involving a dependant.

Transfers of undertakings

Transfer of undertakings regulations were introduced in 1981 as a result of the European Acquired Rights Directive. They are intended to protect the contract of employment and the employment relationship when the undertaking is transferred from one employer to another. If a company is taken over, the Transfer of Undertakings (Protection of Employment) Regulations 2006 state that employees' terms cannot be worsened, including to the point of dismissal, without a good economic, technical or organisational reason.

The issue of when a transfer occurs is, however, a complex one. All rights claims and liabilities, with the exception of pension rights, are transferred, including non-contractual rights.

In the case of *DJM International Limited* v. *Nicholas* ([1996] ICR 214) it was held that liability for an act of sex discrimination transferred from the transferor company to the transferee company. The Employment Appeal Tribunal held that the issue was not whether the alleged act of sex discrimination was in respect of a particular contract, but whether it was in respect of a person employed in the undertaking transferred.

Working time

The Working Time Regulations of 1998 implement the European Working Time Directive and provide for:

- a limit of an average 48 hours a week on the hours a worker can be required to work
- 5.6 weeks' paid leave a year
- 11 consecutive hours' rest in any 24-hour period
- a 20-minute rest break if the working day is longer than six hours
- one day off each week
- a limit on the normal working hours of night workers to an average eight hours in any 24-hour period, and an entitlement for night workers to receive regular health assessments.

The individual worker is able to opt out of the 48-hour week and there is provision determining the rules by collective agreements.

Employees who are officials of unions recognised by the employer are entitled to paid time off during working hours for trade union activities. Employees are entitled to be permitted time off without pay for a number of public duties such as local authorities.

Young employees who are not receiving full-time education are entitled to time off to study for certain qualifications.

Someone who has been employed for two years or more and is under notice of dismissal is entitled to reasonable time off during working hours to look for new work.

Whistle-blowing

Whistle-blowing is when a worker reports suspected wrongdoing at work. Officially this is called 'making a disclosure in the public interest'. A worker can report things that are not right, are illegal or if anyone at work is neglecting their duties, including:

- someone's health and safety is in danger
- damage to the environment
- a criminal offence
- the company is not obeying the law (eg by not having the right insurance)
- covering up wrongdoing.

The worker should check his or her employment contract or ask if the company has a whistle-blowing procedure. If the employee feels able to do so, he or she should contact the employer about the issue the employee wants to report. If the employee feels that he or she cannot tell the employer, the employee should contact a prescribed person or body, such as the Financial Conduct Authority in the case of the financial services sector. If the employee is dismissed, there are certain types of whistle-blowing eligible for protection under the Enterprise and Regulatory Reform Act 2013, basically those noted above, which are held to be in the public interest if so decided in the particular case by an employment tribunal.

The legal framework of collective bargaining

This has been a highly controversial area in British industrial history, and the legislation governing it has been subject to considerable change in the last 40 or so years, just as the union movement has lost power and membership. Indeed, perhaps no other country has seen greater change in its industrial relations framework than the UK, with a move away from collective procedures as the basis for relations between management and labour to one based much more on individual rights. As a result, the very term 'industrial relations' has largely disappeared and been replaced by 'employment relations', as used in this book.

One aspect of this change is that the rules governing the right to strike, a key part of collective bargaining power, have been significantly tightened and are now primarily codified in the Trade Unions and Labour Relations (Consolidation) Act 1992. In order for a group of workers to take strike action, they must:

- hold a ballot of the workforce who will go on strike
- inform the employer of the timing and duration of the strike
- not conduct the industrial action for a purpose unrelated to terms and conditions of the workers' employment contract
- not take industrial action against anyone but the employer of the affected workers
- remain peaceful when conducting picket lines.

The consequence for breach of these rules is that a trade union will be liable for damages to the employer for the cost of the industrial action, and that an injunction may be issued against the industrial action going ahead.

A trade union must be certified as independent by the certification officer and must be recognised by an employer in order to enjoy legal privileges in the area of collective bargaining. Establishing an appropriate bargaining unit is a key prerequisite for the recognition procedure and is carried out by the Central Arbitration Committee (CAC), which also determines whether the union has the support of a majority of workers within the bargaining unit. The CAC can also be used for a procedure of derecognition, and for enforcing the disclosure of information for collective bargaining.

Collective agreements are not generally enforceable and, indeed, are conclusively presumed not to have been intended by the parties to be legally enforceable contracts unless the agreement is in writing and contains a provision which states that the parties intend it to be enforceable.

All forms of industrial action are likely to constitute a breach of an individual's contract of employment. Inducing the breach of a contract, whether of employment or commercial, is a key dimension of the law on industrial action. However, there is statutory immunity against tort challenges where the industrial action takes place in contemplation or furtherance of a trade dispute. Unions and their officials can benefit from immunity only if the union has authorised the industrial action after there has been majority support for the action in a ballot of the members concerned not more than four weeks before the start of the action.

Other actions with possible legal consequences include picketing, intimidation, conspiracy, inducing a breach of a statutory duty and interference with business by unlawful means.

There are now also substantial legal controls on the relationship between trade unions and their members.

Wider rights in the employment context

The Human Rights Act 1998 incorporates Article 8(1) of the European Convention on Human Rights. Areas that may have an influence on employment law are the right to respect for private and family life, freedom of thought, conscience and religion, freedom of expression and freedom of assembly and association.

The Data Protection Act 1998 also arose from European sources and provides protection against misuse of personal information by giving rights to individuals about whom information is recorded on computers.

The Access to Medical Reports Act 1988 provides a right of access to any medical report relating to an individual which has been or will be supplied by a medical practitioner for employment or insurance purposes. Nevertheless, medical practitioners who carry out such assessments owe a duty of care to the employer who is relying on the report, rather than to the employee.

Under the Rehabilitation of Offenders Act 1974, where a person who has been convicted of an offence and has served a sentence in custody must, after a period of between five and 10 years, be treated as if the offence had never been committed. This means that the candidate is not obliged to reveal any such sentence to a prospective employer. Certain categories of employee, including accountants, lawyers, teachers, those in the medical profession and those who work with persons under the age of 18, can be asked to disclose any previous offences.

The Pensions Act 2008 holds that, as from October 2012, every 'jobholder' (defined as a worker, aged 16 to 75, with wages between £5,035 and £33,540) must be automatically enrolled by the employer in an occupational pension scheme, unless they choose to opt out.

The Regulation of Investigatory Powers Act 2000 and Telecommunications (Lawful Business Practice) (Interception of Communications) Regulations 2000 state that an employer cannot check personal emails *at all* without the sender's consent, even from a work email account. It may check business emails to assess whether a crime has been committed or unauthorised activity has occurred, but only in strictly defined circumstances.

Under the Information and Consultation of Employees Regulations 2004, companies with more than 50 employees must inform their workforce about major economic issues in their enterprise, and should consult about major changes, particularly redundancies. The Jobseekers Act 1995 provides a jobseeker's allowance, dependent on the claimant's availability for work and actively seeking work.

The Retirement Age Regulations, which came into effect in October 2011, mean that the default retirement age (formerly 65) has been phased out – most people can now work for as long as they want to. Retirement age is when an employee chooses to retire. Most businesses do not set a compulsory retirement age for their employees. If an employee chooses to work longer he or she cannot be discriminated against. However, some employers can set a compulsory retirement age if they can clearly justify it. It is an employee's responsibility to discuss when and how to retire with the employer.

The Immigration, Asylum and Nationality Act 2006 obliges employers to prevent illegal working in the UK by carrying out prescribed document checks on people before employing them. These checks have been strengthened by changes to the scheme in May 2014.

Activities

1. Bring together the organisation's range of rules for all the areas which may have legal consequences under employment law, so that you are aware of their existence if you need to refer to them.
2. What does your organisation do to ensure that it is up to date with changes in aspects of employment law?

References

Acas *Annual Reports*. London, Acas.

Acas *Newsletters*. London, Acas.

Employment Rights Act 1996 s123. Available on-line at www.legislation.gov.uk/ukpga/1996/18/section/123 [accessed 16 January 2015].

10 Operating in a world of change

Introduction

You will recall that we began this book by introducing the theme of change, and gave a substantial range of dimensions in which change is taking place. Indeed, most of this book has been about managing change of one sort or another – recruiting new staff, looking at innovative ways in which people's jobs can be improved, managing changes in individual and group behaviour, leading the changing processes that teams go through, managing people's development, coping with changes in people's working lives, right through to the changes in employment law that featured in the previous chapter.

Change comes in all shapes and sizes. In some contexts there is an omnipresent series of incremental changes, with an occasional bigger one; in other contexts it arrives totally unexpectedly – earthquakes can be metaphorical as well as literal; in others again it results out of a period of uncertainty; and in yet others it is planned over a long period. It is therefore appropriate that this concluding chapter deals more explicitly with the challenge of change.

Acas, in its booklet *How to Manage Change* (2010), notes that major change in organisations happens approximately every three years and that minor change is constant. Previous generations have not thought in these terms; rather that change is interspersed with long periods of stability, so that change is the exception rather than the rule and the future becomes less and less like the past. Coping with modern change means that organisations can no longer expect stability. If its major customer goes out of business or takes its custom elsewhere or a new competitor enters the market, the organisation's financial situation can plummet overnight. CEOs all too often see it as not only being their prerogative but their obligation to introduce change. And not at all infrequently, the following sort of scenario appears.

> 'Things aren't going to be the same when the merger happens. Denos is going to be the dominant partner because it is very hierarchical – very structured with strong financial controls. We're big, but very decentralised. Each of the business units do things their own way – lots of autonomy, although they are supported from head office. We're losing 100 staff here but

Denos employees will come in with a completely different cultural background. I can see all the good work we've done over the last few years being lost as well' (manager in pharmaceuticals company).

For managers, change means keeping a close eye on both internal performance and external developments and, in many cases, having not just to manage but to lead organisational restructuring. Although some people see change as a challenge and an opportunity, many others fear it. They see change as threatening because organisational change usually involves people in changing their existing working practices and processes and even their attitudes towards the job and others in the organisation. And often they are right to fear it. There is hardly a significant organisation that has not undergone substantial changes in the last decade. The repercussions, moreover, have often been very painful. Consider the different words and phrases which are used to describe restructuring – hard words such as downsizing, delayering, headcount reduction, terminating employment, redundancy – even though the official front is all about valuing contributions, counselling and relocating. This does not mean that change is undesirable or unnecessary, but it does mean that it is not easy when it can substantially affect people's lives.

Even as a front-line manager, you have a choice. The choice is not between managing change or not managing change but between managing change through people or despite people. In virtually every case, we argue, the former is more successful, and we also argue that it is at your level that the difference between success and failure can be most critical.

The role of the front-line manager becomes particularly important in periods of change as the face of the organisation and the person to whom employees look to satisfy their personal concerns. This is a time when leadership becomes even more important because of the inevitable 'visibility ... consistency ... accessibility ... decisiveness ... clarity' (Acas 2010: 19). If management is acceptable in periods of stability, leadership is necessary in periods of change, right down to the level of the front-line manager. This is a time when anxiety and stress are most prevalent and the front-line manager is the first recipient of these feelings. For front-line managers, change is often imposed from higher up in the organisation but they have to activate the change on the ground; this can be a difficult job, requiring real leadership skills. Change does not just happen because those above give an order. Moreover, there may well be changes which need initiating at a relatively low level.

In this chapter, we start with what might be called the mechanics of change but conclude by examining the philosophy of change in a wider context:

- pressures for change
- challenges in change
- levels of change
- initiating and planning for change
- stages of change

- communicating change
- responses to change
- coping with reactions to change
- a philosophy of change
- last thoughts.

Pressures for change

Pressures for change usually come from outside the organisation in the first place, from changes in the organisation's environment. Some can be identified a long way ahead, such as demographic changes, whilst others come out of the blue, as literally happened in the September 2001 attacks on the World Trade Center in New York, or unfold rapidly on an uncomprehending world, as with the global financial crisis of 2008. Technology is a constant of change, although not necessarily in a predictable way. These external pressures can combine with pressures from inside the organisation, such as the need to increase productivity or improve performance or to restructure work or the organisation. Although both will be considered separately here, they are nearly always interlinked.

External pressures for change

The rapidly changing environment in which organisations exist in today's world creates continuous pressure for change. These pressures can be categorised as social, technological, political, economic, environmental and market-related, as shown in figure 10.1. Many general trends and pressures in these areas were identified in

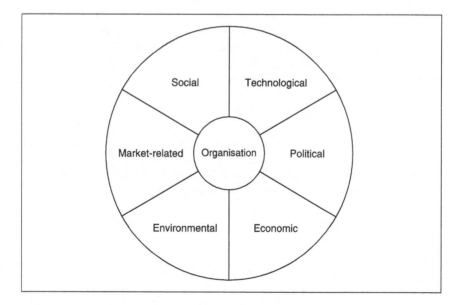

Figure 10.1 External pressures for change.

Chapter 1, but many others will be more specific to industries or even individual organisations.

In Russia and other parts of Eastern Europe, subsidised canteens and free meat supplies used to be the top priorities for workers in Western-owned companies. These have now been overtaken by low-interest loans, personal credit cards, car allowances and medical benefits.

At the 33rd World Santa Claus and Christmas Elves Congress, held in Copenhagen, delegates debated the ethics of the internet and learned how to set up their own websites. 'We have to see the new technology as an opportunity,' said Ib Rasmussen, organiser of the Congress. 'We have to say to children that there is not one single Father Christmas, but a well-organized staff of Santas and elves' (Follett 1996).

Applying these ideas to your own experience

Take each of the six areas in figure 10.1 and identify a pressure that has had an impact on your organisation. How have they affected your job and those of your staff?

Internal pressures for change

Pressures for change from within an organisation can be 'top-down' or 'bottom-up'; that is, they can come from the leader of the organisation or senior management or from the organisation's employees. If you are relatively junior in your organisation, you have probably experienced top-down change. Your reaction to it will have depended on how it was communicated to you, how closely it affected you personally and whether you were consulted about the change and its effects at any point. Except in times of real crisis, top-down change is usually resented by those it affects lower down in the organisation.

Radical change, whether as a result of external or internal pressures or a combination of these, often has to be imposed from the top when a chief executive or management team is charged with turning around a failing organisation. Radical change is usually engendered by strong external pressures and the likelihood of collapse unless drastic action is taken. It usually involves large-scale redundancies or relocation of staff and will only be successful if senior management is committed to the strategy and staff are kept informed of what is happening.

Top-down change needs to be handled sensitively and involve as many people as possible lower down in the organisation if it is going to be accepted without resistance. Channels of communication, upward and downward, need to be effective and staff need to be kept informed about plans for change. Where time and other pressures allow, as much consultation as is possible about the way the change will be implemented and its effects on individuals and groups will result in a higher rate of acceptance and even positive enthusiasm. Consider the following example.

In 1995, Mobil Oil moved its London office to Milton Keynes. Within 24 hours of the announcement of the relocation in November 1994, employees were given a presentation by senior management explaining the benefits of the move. The following day, a Saturday, a video package arrived at each employee's home showing the new offices and the Milton Keynes area. Consultants were brought in and visited individual staff to discuss the problems they faced, including the selling of their property. Home owners who agreed to move were offered a guaranteed price by the consultants who then took over the responsibility for selling the property. Half of the employees agreed to relocate and 60 per cent of these moved to the Milton Keynes area. Those who chose not to relocate received redundancy payments and full outplacement support (Merrick 1995).

Pressure from staff can be very effective in creating change, providing senior management is prepared to take notice. If ignored, it can degenerate into dissatisfaction and even result in industrial action. Again, consider this example.

Employees at Company X had petitioned for longer rest periods for some time, but their arguments were ignored. Eventually, their grievance reached the level where the union was brought in and a long and bitter battle with the employers was fought before going to arbitration. The arbitrator found for the employees and the company was forced to increase rest times accordingly. However, since the dispute had involved the staff in working to rule over a period of several weeks, the company had lost several major customers during this time and its financial outlook was bleak.

The challenges in change

Change conjures up words like 'exhilarating', 'exciting', 'challenging' or others such as 'frightening', 'exhausting', 'unnecessary'. In fact, many people feel very threatened by change. People who have been made redundant can usually blame this on some kind of change – a change in working practices, in company structure, in market demand and so on. People who are stuck somewhere in the middle of an organisation can blame this on not having the right skills at the right time. All too often change takes place without the involvement of many of those affected by it, creating fear and suspicion of the unknown.

On the other hand, change offers opportunities – the chance to learn new skills, for example, and working with new people and new technology. Job satisfaction may be increased through improved working conditions and practices and better, more efficient use of your skills and time. New or changed jobs can bring increased status and responsibility; reward systems can be improved and made more relevant.

Even though being made redundant may be traumatic at the time, it may seem, in retrospect, it forced you to accept the reality of the situation and change yourself for the better (although it must be noted that for many people who are made redundant there are no second chances). The MacLeod Report (2009: 16) reported that nine out of ten of the key barriers to the success of change programmes are people-related.

Applying these ideas to your own experience

Think about your own reactions to change and jot down the words you would use to describe recent changes at work and the way you feel about them. Can you think of some of the opportunities that change can offer to those who are involved in it at your place of work?

With all these pressures on organisations to change, you would expect there to be other factors that constrain change from taking place. This, of course, is true. Factors which limit change and can prevent it from occurring could include financial or other resource constraints, people's attitudes and resistance to change and legal or other restrictions. In 1951 the psychologist Kurt Lewin devised a model which has been called 'force field analysis' as a way of looking at change situations. Lewin called pressures for change 'driving forces'; these included any external or internal pressures but might also include individuals or groups of people. 'Restraining forces' are Lewin's term for factors that are preventing change from taking place and these too can include individuals or groups. When the driving and restraining forces for change are equal, then a state of equilibrium exists – in other words, nothing happens. If the relative strengths of either the driving or restraining forces change,

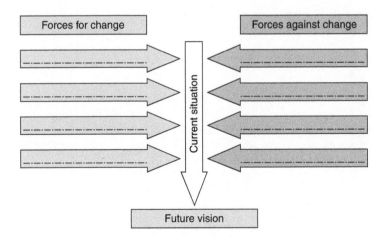

Figure 10.2 Forcefield analysis.

© Acas, Euston Tower, 286 Euston Road, London NW1 3JJ

then there is activity, which may consist either of change or of a deeper entrenchment into preserving the status quo. In any situation, each of the arrows would have a title that described the individual driving or restraining force, and each would carry with it greater or lesser significance.

You need to identify the driving and restraining forces of any change you are proposing to make in order to analyse how successful – or otherwise – it may be. If you find that the restraining forces are equal to, or stronger than, the driving forces, you will need to strengthen the driving forces. This could be accomplished by providing more resources, financial or human, to add to the driving forces you have already identified. It could also, and often more easily, be achieved by reducing the strength of the restraining forces. You could, for example, decrease fear of change as a restraining force by involving people in the plans for change and reducing their level of anxiety about its outcome.

Applying these ideas to your own experience

Take the pressures for change and the pressures against change in a situation you know well and set them against each other in a force field analysis, drawing lines of what you consider to be the appropriate thickness to represent their relative importance.

Levels of change

The length of time needed for managing change and the degree of difficulty you should expect are both directly related to the level of the change which is being proposed, as shown in figure 10.3. Changes can be made at the individual, group

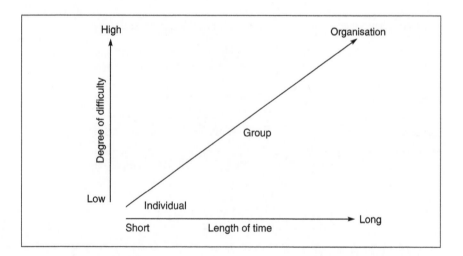

Figure 10.3 Levels of change.

and organisational levels and a change which affects a single individual can be expected to be simpler to manage and to take less time than one which affects groups of people or the whole organisation. This is, however, rather simplistic since making a small change to the job of one individual can quite often affect others. For example, if I changed from giving work to my secretary in manuscript to dictating it, her method of work would change but the effect would probably be restricted to her alone. If, however, I asked her to work from home, such a change would involve others in supplying her with appropriate equipment, making arrangements for cover for my telephone calls when I was absent and, probably, widespread reactions from other secretarial and clerical staff concerning their working conditions; the level of the change would not be at the individual level but at the group and, even possibly, the organisational levels. A major consideration in planning change is to identify its effects at all levels before putting it into practice.

Change in the NHS

One of the most ambitious and comprehensive programmes of change ever introduced is in the National Health Service in England, most of which took effect on 1 April 2013. The NHS Change Model brought together collective improvement knowledge and experience from across the NHS, developed with hundreds of senior leaders, clinicians, commissioners, providers and improvement activists across the NHS by the application of eight components.

Leadership for change

The evidence suggests that the leadership style and philosophy that is most likely to deliver large scale change is one that generates a commitment to a shared purpose through collaboration.

Spread of innovation

We need to accelerate the speed and extent of the spread and adoption of innovation in order to deliver the cost savings required, whilst improving the quality of care we deliver. This will mean more active sharing of successful innovations with others across the NHS and more being prepared to learn from others and adopt innovations from elsewhere into our own practice.

Improvement methodology

Using an evidence-based improvement methodology ensures that the change will be delivered in a planned, proven way that follows established methods. The improvement methodology is the game plan. There is a range of proven methodologies available to support different kinds of change, with a particular emphasis on large scale change across systems, not just process improvement.

Rigorous delivery

The evidence suggests that an effective approach for the delivery of change and the monitoring of progress towards planned objectives are essential to making that change a reality. It provides greater financial and quality control of the change to deliver benefits of strategic importance. Without rigorous delivery other elements of the change model will fail.

Transparent measurement

Measuring the outcome of change continuously and transparently is crucial to providing evidence that the change is happening and the desired results are being achieved.

System drivers

When we want to change something, whether it is just something small or the way a whole health care system works, we know that we need conditions to be right if what we change is going to both work as we wanted it to and also stay changed for the future. Key to both of these is whether the broad conditions for change – the system drivers – can be lined up to support what we are trying to do. These drivers might take the form of incentives for change or specific standards to be achieved if penalties are to be avoided.

Engagement to mobilise

This involves five energies: psychological, social, spiritual, intellectual and physical.

www.changemodel.nhs.uk.

Initiating and planning for change

One of the most difficult but nevertheless most important dimensions of change is to decide when it is desirable and how it should be achieved and then planning for its introduction. It is possible that a very sudden event, such as the attacks on the World Trade Center, imposes change, or alternatively that change slowly evolves, almost without anybody noticing it. But these two extremes are exceptional. In the vast majority of cases, change results from decisions that it is desirable, and somebody initiates the process. Even if the process of change is highly consultative, somebody usually has to begin it, and if, which again is the norm, that person is a manager, it helps greatly that a good deal of analysis and preparation predates any proposals. There are arguably five separate issues that need to be considered.

- Define the problem. Is the change really necessary, or at least desirable? Change for the sake of it, as sometimes seems to employees to have happened in organisations from the 1980s and increasingly since, is very wearing and creates cynicism amongst those it affects. There is a need to recognise that continuity, as well as change, has merits; indeed, constant change can be destructive, because people can only take so much. On the other hand, it is obviously undesirable to wait until it is too late, and change is imposed by people or circumstances. Some sort of cost–benefit analysis, even in the light of various unknowns, needs to be done here.
- Can the change being envisaged be achieved? If there are serious problems, is there a better way?
- What needs to be changed and what not? It is quite easy to aim for more change than is really necessary.
- What are the potential outcomes? This may well involve scenario planning.
- Finally, what is the optimum achievable outcome? Identifying this is by no means easy, and indeed requires a vision of the future, an attribute of most successful leaders, but not something that everyone possesses.

Reflecting on the last point above, the role of leadership is a key one in change. Leadership is needed at all stages of change, and the type of leadership may be different at different stages, but it is arguably most needed when initiating and planning change. Without a vision of the future, it will be very difficult to communicate with and enthuse others about the need for change.

Stages of change

When a change is taking place, at any of the levels described above, it needs to go through various stages. Change management is a common feature of organisational systems and many companies have their own approaches. A simple and easily understandable approach to stages, also identified by Kurt Lewin (1951), involves unfreezing, changing and refreezing.

'Unfreezing' relates to the need to change existing attitudes towards working practices and processes before the change can begin to take place – it is the stage of preparing the ground. This is when communication about any proposed change is vital if people are to understand and support it. This may mean holding open meetings at which plans for change can be discussed by everyone concerned, or creating a newsletter to inform people, particularly those who may be involved and interested but who cannot attend meetings. It may mean holding one-to-one talks with key people and arranging for more widespread communication and reassurance on a cascade basis. If the change is going to involve people acquiring new skills, arrangements for training should fall into this stage as well. It is also a time when plans may need to be modified in the light of consultation with other people.

'Changing' is the implementation stage, and its success will depend on the thoroughness of planning and preparation. It is common to find that the implementation stage takes much longer than people expected and that time scales are often unrealistic. Moreover, problems can occur at the stage of implementation which had not been identified at the planning stage, such as poor coordination, the overestimation of people's abilities to adjust, inadequate training or that the plans are too rigid in a context which needs some degree of flexibility. Indeed, factors outside the organisation's control, such as legal, governmental or economic changes, can have an adverse effect on implementation.

'Refreezing', the final stage of change, is one of consolidation. Even when a change appears to have been planned and implemented successfully, problems can occur. For example, new equipment may have been effectively introduced and its operators trained in its use. Those responsible for the change, however, could pat themselves on the back too soon. Operators can too easily revert to old working practices despite the new technology unless there is ongoing monitoring once the change is in place. Not until it has become incorporated into the working culture can the change be said to have been 'refrozen'. Refreezing, therefore, involves continuous evaluation of the success of the implementation stage. Problems or dissatisfaction may occur after implementation and these need to be identified and dealt with promptly to prevent further disruption.

This three-stage model is, of course, rather simplistic in suggesting that change starts and stops in coherent activities and in not taking enough account of the tactical aspects of the process. Kotter (2012) has written his seminal book *Leading Change* around eight stages, which incorporate separate processes:

- pressures for change
- challenges in change
- levels of change
- establishing a sense of urgency
- creating the guiding coalition
- developing a vision and strategy
- communicating the change vision
- empowering employees in broad-based action
- generating short-term wins
- consolidating gains and producing more change
- anchoring new approaches in the culture.

Communicating change

Communicating the issues in change effectively is a critical part of making change successful, and the following points are helpful in achieving this:

- Do your homework on the issues.

- Think about the message you are going to deliver from the point of view of your audience.
- If necessary, customise the message for different audiences.
- Also consider different media: thus, if a lot of detailed information needs to be digested, email might be better than a talk which loses people through too much detail. But always enable people to ask questions, which usually means a meeting.
- Look for feedback and try to respond to it, if possible building on what has been said.
- Use plain language.
- Remember that it is not just the words that you use that make an impact, but the tone of voice and the body language. Indeed, it has been estimated that the reception of a message is broken down by: 55 per cent body language; 38 per cent tone of voice; and only 7 per cent words (Thompson 2011). The physical context can make a difference too.
- Don't promise what you can't be sure of delivering.
- If possible, break the issues down with something like a SWOT analysis. Accept that there are weaknesses as well as strengths, threats as well as opportunities. Most of your audience are going to work this out for themselves anyway.
- Remember that occasions such as the introduction of change require leadership; be more than just a messenger.

Responses to change

The extent to which individuals are likely to be resistant, indifferent or supportive towards change depends on the degree to which they perceive the change will affect them personally and their way of working. People will feel threatened by change if they think it is going to affect their pay, their status, their place of work, their chances of advancement or any other aspect of their job which is important to them. They may also be resistant to change because they have suffered a surfeit of changes at work; there comes a point when people seek some kind of stability, rationally or not, in an environment of constant change.

People almost naturally appear to resist change. It seems to be part of human nature to create norms with which people feel comfortable and, if these norms are threatened, resistance occurs. Often people feel genuinely apprehensive when they hear things are likely to change, and this apprehension increases if they lack information about what is going to happen.

Kotter and Schlesinger (1979) identified the main reasons why people resisted change as the following.

Parochial self-interest. Subconsciously, most people put their own welfare before that of the organisation. If they perceive a change as being in the organisation's interests but either not in, or, worse, actively against their own interests, they will resist it. If the change, for example, is perceived to be going to result in lower pay, loss of autonomy, power or identity, or indeed loss of any other factor of value to the individual, he or she is likely to oppose it. In addition, since most change is intended to increase efficiency, it may well be seen as requiring more work for the staff involved. This opposition, if shared with others, may result in the growth of pressure groups to prevent the change from taking place.

Misunderstanding. If communication about a proposed change has not been adequate, people are likely to misunderstand its implications for them and their jobs. If there is a lack of trust between those responsible, or held responsible, for the change and those who are going to be affected by it, misunderstanding is linked to mistrust. Rumour and conjecture are likely to result, often leading to increased resistance. This situation is likely where there are uncertainties about the proposals, or people do not have sufficient warning about what is being suggested.

Different assessments of the situation. Enthusiasts for change often assume that everyone shares their vision of its benefits. In fact, this is rarely true since individuals have different aspirations, values and expectations. Shared assessment of the benefits of change will only result if everyone is in possession of the same amount of relevant information about it. Even then, individuals may not share the same values. If the change is going to result in increased pay for everyone, for example, only those who value pay highly are likely to see this as a benefit; others may perceive disadvantages in loss of free time or reduced overtime which accompany the increase in pay. The danger in making these kinds of generalised assumptions is that there is likely to be open disagreement with the plans for change.

Low tolerance of change. If people have strong needs for security and stability, they are likely to resist change through apprehension that it will threaten these cornerstones of their existence. They may fear that they will find it difficult to learn new skills or work practices or that they may lose the companionship of their work colleagues through relocation or reallocation of work. They will oppose the idea of change, either openly or by making excuses for why they do not support it. Reassurance and support are essential for people with these apprehensions.

Applying these ideas to your own experience

Think about a change at work in which you have been involved. Did you or your colleagues experience any resistance to change? Was this resistance caused by any of the reasons above?

Coping with reactions to change

Kotter and Schlesinger (1979) identified a number of ways by which resistance to change might be reduced, noting the advantages and disadvantages of each.

Education. Educating people about the change beforehand and ensuring that ideas about change are fully communicated to everyone who is likely to be affected by it will help people to understand why the change is necessary. It is particularly effective when resistance is based on inadequate or inaccurate information and when those who are responsible for initiating the change need the support of those who oppose it. However, any adequate programme of education and communication is costly in terms of time and effort and relies on a relationship of trust between those driving and those restraining the change.

Participation and involvement. Top-down imposition of change is often unsuccessful because those designing the change have failed to take into account the knowledge and expertise of the people at whom the change is aimed. Where information from others is necessary, they need to be invited to participate in planning the change. Otherwise, they can create considerable resistance at the stage of implementation.

In general, participation and involvement of everyone who will be affected by the change leads to commitment and support for its implementation. It can, however, be an enormously time-consuming process and needs careful management. If the change needs to occur in a very short space of time, it may take too long to involve other people.

Facilitation and support. When fear and apprehension of change are the main reasons for resistance, managers need to be supportive to the problems of adjustment their staff are experiencing. They might spend time reassuring people about their apprehensions and explaining the need for change. They could also provide additional support in the form of training. All this takes time and commitment from the manager as well as patience, since fears of change may be deeply rooted and difficult to remove.

Negotiation and agreement. In some cases, opposition to change can be so powerful that incentives need to be offered if the change is to go ahead. These may take the form of individual incentives, such as promotion or a generous early retirement package, or it might involve negotiating with the union so that employees receive higher pay or other appropriate rewards in return for a change in working hours. Such negotiating tactics can prove to be expensive for the organisation and a manager who resorts too easily to negotiation may be seen as a target for blackmail by other resistant groups.

Manipulation and cooption. Where, for example, an individual has considerable influence over others and, thus, power to increase resistance, managers may resort to 'coopting' that person onto their side. This is often done by giving the person some attractive role in the design and implementation of the change so that he or she is publicly seen to be supporting it. Because it is a devious way of reducing resistance, it is also often unsuccessful and can lead to greater opposition.

Explicit and implicit coercion. As with the last method, this too is not to be recommended except as a last resort. It can involve forcing people to accept a change, riding roughshod over opposition, usually because the reasons for the change are overwhelmingly stronger than any resistance to it and, no matter what tactics are employed, the change is going to be unpopular. It requires considerable personal authority and power on the part of the person who is implementing the change, as well as the ability to cope with prolonged dissatisfaction during the third stage of change.

Change agents. When massive change at the organisational level needs to be undertaken, it is often necessary to bring in a 'change agent'. Organisations prefer stability and, like individuals, resist change because of the upheaval it will cause. Senior managers within the organisation are not usually the most adept at planning radical change since they themselves have a stake in preserving the *status quo*. The change agent, on the other hand, may be an independent consultant or may be recruited as a full-time member of the organisation's staff.

The change agent brings a fresh and generally unbiased approach to designing a programme of change. He or she works with members of the organisation at all levels, identifying the problems and helping them to generate solutions. Often, the change agent will take responsibility for implementing the solutions, particularly if they are likely to be unpopular with large sections of staff.

With any change you are involved in planning and implementing, you can expect there to be a certain amount of resistance. The secret lies in identifying why and where this is most likely to occur and adopting a strategy in advance to cope with it. The strategy is likely to be influenced by the circumstances: the degree of resistance, the power of the initiator and the time-scale available. At one end of the spectrum a more directive approach is likely to work, where there is a clear view of what is to be done, little involvement with people and resistance can be brushed aside; at the other end a more consultative and slower approach is indicated, where there is a good deal of involvement of other people, and where there is a less definitive commitment to a particular outcome.

Applying these ideas to your own experience

In the last change in which you were involved, which of the above strategies was used to achieve the change? Why was this particular strategy adopted?

A final issue in change that is all too often forgotten is evaluation of how well the change works. It is difficult because new factors start interposing themselves in the situation and interfere with any attempt to measure the outcomes of the change itself. Nevertheless, it is important to try, because there are almost certainly important lessons that can be learned and applied to the next attempt to pursue change. If evaluation is going to be successful, it is important that a process for carrying it out is built into the original plans.

A philosophy of change

We finish with a look at the wider context and longer-term perspective on change, taking up the views of John Kotter and his book *Leading Change* (2012), which was chosen by *Time Magazine* as one of the 25 most influential books on management. The book covers many dimensions of change such as power, vision and strategy, and failure as well as success, but we want to focus on and expand three themes which have particular relevance for front-line managers and represent an important philosophy underpinning successful change.

The first of these is lifelong learning. 'Leadership and lifelong learning' is the title of Kotter's last chapter, and in it he reviews his own misconception about the traditional model of leadership, about which he admitted that 'the older model is nearly oblivious to the power and potential of lifelong learning' (2012: 184). Lifelong learners keep learning as they did in full-time education and are able to develop skills that they previously lacked. Nor are these skills a result of a particular position in the hierarchy; they can be developed from almost anywhere. Lifelong learning creates people who can keep up with and adapt to a rapidly changing environment and thus learn to be leaders. Kotter quotes his study of the Harvard MBA class of 1974, in which he analysed what were the key factors identified with success; they emerged as competitive drive and lifelong learning. Lifelong learning is partly about upgrading one's technical and professional skills, as many professional institutes routinely require. But it is also about learning through listening, observing, reflecting, trying new things and thinking beyond the confines of the immediate context, producing what Kotter calls 'the power of compounded growth' (2012: 189). Front-line managers can do this; indeed anyone can do it, although few do.

The second concept is broad-based empowerment as a key attribute of the organisation of the future. Kotter conceives of it being organised 'with the expectation that management will lead, lower-level employees will manage' (2012: 181). This takes us back to the concept of self-managing teams as discussed in Chapter 6 and how giving them the power to manage themselves makes them more effective and gives managers, including front-line managers, more time to think, reflect and learn, rather than being continually obsessed with micromanagement. So many managers complain: 'I never have time to think'. Empowerment means that employees can develop under-utilised skills and themselves appreciate the rapidly changing context in which they work. This appreciation is something that organisations of the future will require as part of the change process, not least because empowered workers will find the need for change easier to understand.

The third theme is delegation. This means not just delegation to front-line managers but beyond them. Delegation is a very necessary part of the distributed leadership which we also discussed in Chapter 6. Without delegation it is not possible for front-line managers to lead. Delegation is also part of the flatter structures, more inclusive information systems, management support systems and more widely available training systems that flexible organisations need. Delegation, if properly done, is not abdication of responsibility, because the senior remains responsible for all the work done. It can save money and time, help in building skills and motivate people. Front-line managers arguably stand at the key standpoint of making delegation effective, because without their input, good intentions die. The opposite of effective delegation is micromanagement, where a manager provides too much input, direction and review of delegated work.

Activities

This may involve consolidating some of the answers as you went through the chapter. Think of a change at work in which you were personally involved.

1. Identify:

    (a) any external pressures for change
    (b) any internal pressures for change.

2. At which level(s) did the change take place:

    (a) individual
    (b) group
    (c) organisational?

3. Draw a force field analysis of the change, identifying the driving and restraining forces and indicating their relative strengths.
4. What amount of preparatory analysis was carried out?
5. What efforts were made:

    (a) to unfreeze the change
    (b) to effect the change
    (c) to refreeze or consolidate the change?

6. Was there any resistance to the idea of change or to the change itself? What were the underlying causes of this resistance?
7. What methods were used to reduce or overcome any resistance to change?
8. Was there any evaluation of the change after the event?

Last thoughts

Even since the previous edition of this book, the rate of change seems to have accelerated, and some of it has been most unwelcome, such as the global financial crisis of 2008. We referred to the volatility, uncertainty, complexity and ambiguity of the environment on the first page of the book (this is commonly referred to using the acronym VUCA). But one thing is constant, that front-line managers are going to play an important role in making change successful, since it is the front-line manager who translates the organisational issues into personal issues for staff and is the first port of call in helping the employees to respond to change.

We would like to leave you with a few last thoughts from the book:

1. Remember the importance of behaving ethically and professionally; employees look to you as the face of the organisation.

2. Remember the soft skills and the importance of emotional intelligence, especially empathy in relating to how other people feel.
3. Remember the importance of learning constantly from experience and making a commitment to lifelong learning.
4. If there is one thing that we have tried to emphasise that differentiates this edition from its predecessors, it is that in this modern context, front-line managers have a leadership as well as merely a management role to play.

Finally, here are six golden rules of being effective as a front-line manager (Taylor 2014: 295)

*   Give praise where praise is due.
*   Avoid the perception of favouritism.
*   Talk to every team member regularly.
*   Act when you suspect there are problems.
*   Give people as much autonomy as you possibly can.
*   Involve people in decision-making.

References

Acas, (2010) *How to Manage Change.* Advisory booklet. London, Acas.
Follett C., (1996) '60 sweating santas convene for world congress', *The Moscow Times*, 24 July. Available on-line at: www.themoscowtimes.com/sitemap/free/1996/7/article/60-sweating-santas-convene-for-world-congress/321022.html [accessed 16 January 2015].
Kotter J. P., (2012) *Leading Change.* Boston, Mass., Harvard Business Review Press.
Kotter J. P. and Schlesinger L. A., (1979) 'Choosing strategies for change', *Harvard Business Review*, 57(2): 106–114.
Lewin K., (1951) *Field Theory in Social Science.* London, Harper.
McLeod D. and Clarke M., (2009) *Engaging for Success: Enhancing Performance through Employee Engagement.* London, Department for Business, Innovation and Skills.
Merrick N., (1995) 'The Mobil way to achieve mobility', *People Management*, November, 37–38.
Taylor S., (2014) *Resourcing and Talent Management*, 6th edition. London, Chartered Institute of Personnel and Development.
Thompson J., (2011) 'Is non-verbal communication a numbers game?', *Psychology Today* 30. Available on-line at: www.psychologytoday.com/blog/beyond-words/201109/is-nonverbal-communication-numbers-game [accessed 19 January 2015].

Index

Note: Page numbers in **bold** are for figures, those in *italics* are for tables.

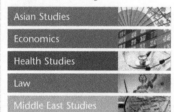